Program Administration Scale

Second Edition

Measuring Early Childhood Leadership and Management

TEACHERS COLLEGE PRESS

TEACHERS COLLEGE | COLUMBIA UNIVERSITY

NEW YORK AND LONDON

Teri N. Talan, J.D., Ed.D., and
Paula Jorde Bloom, Ph.D.

Published by Teachers College Press, 1234 Amsterdam Avenue, New York, NY 10027

Cover photos by Donna Jonas

ISBN 978-0-8077-5245-6

Printed on acid-free paper
Manufactured in the United States of America

Training is available from the McCormick Center for Early Childhood Leadership (McCormickCenter.nl.edu) for practitioners, researchers, and program evaluators to help ensure the most reliable use of the *Program Administration Scale*. Contact Dr. Teri Talan, the McCormick Center for Early Childhood Leadership, National Louis University, 6200 Capitol Drive, Wheeling, Illinois 60090, 800-443-5522, ext. 5060 or teri.talan@nl.edu for further information.

Contents

Acknowledgments

Since the publication of the first edition of the *Program Administration Scale* (PAS) in 2004, we have had the privilege of working with hundreds of early childhood administrators, technical assistance specialists, and policymakers across the United States, Canada, and Singapore. Many of these individuals attended intensive assessor reliability training and became certified PAS assessors so they could collect data for research or quality improvement initiatives. We are so appreciative of the clarifying questions and insightful comments we received at each of these training events. We want to express our gratitude to all the training participants and acknowledge their valuable contribution to this second edition of the *Program Administration Scale*.

The impetus for the PAS came from our work assessing program quality as part of a McCormick Foundation professional development initiative. The experience convinced us of the need for a valid and reliable instrument to measure the quality of leadership and management practices of center-based early care and education programs. The W. Clement and Jessie V. Stone Foundation provided the funding to conduct the initial reliability and validity study of the PAS. We are indebted to both foundations for their continued support of our work and their commitment to improving the quality of early childhood program administration.

We are grateful for the insights we received from experts in the field who helped shape the development of the *Program Administration Scale*. Our heartfelt thanks go to Kay Albrecht, Bee Jay Ciszek, Doug Clark, Dick Clifford, Debby Cryer, Eileen Eisenberg, Jana Fleming, Lois Gamble, John Gunnarson, Thelma Harms, Judy Harris Helm, Kendra Kett, Stacy Kim, Jackie Legg, Sam Meisels, Anne Mitchell, Gwen Morgan, Kathie Raiborn, Susan Sponheimer, Marilyn Sprague-Smith, and Lana Weiner.

Appreciation also goes to the research team involved in our initial reliability and validity study of the PAS—Jill Bella, Linda Butkovich, Lisa Downey, Shirley Flath, Kathy Hardy, Karen May, Gale Reinitz, Sara Starbuck, and Cass Wolfe. The staff at the Illinois Network of Child Care Resource and Referral Agencies and the Metropolitan Chicago Information Center were particularly helpful during the sample selection process for our initial reliability study.

We also want to recognize the certified PAS assessors who conducted the assessments in 25 states that were used in the national reliability and validity study reported in this second edition. These valued colleagues are too numerous to name, but without their important contributions, the development of national norms would not have been possible.

We are extremely grateful for the statistical support we received from Diana Schaack. Her assistance with coding and analyzing the data from our national sample saved us considerable time. Thanks as well to Heather Knapp and Tanya Rafraf who helped with data entry, Donna Jonas who did the layout of the final document, and Kathy Rousseau who provided a critical eye in proofing the contents.

It has been a real pleasure to work with the editors and production team at Teachers College Press. Our deep appreciation goes to Marie Ellen Larcada for keeping us focused and navigating this project through to completion.

And finally, there are three members of our PAS Review Team at the McCormick Center for Early Childhood Leadership that merit special recognition—Jill Bella, Linda Butkovich, and Robyn Kelton. Their expertise about the nuances of the PAS and their tireless efforts in responding to questions from the field, supporting "end users," and overseeing our PAS certification system provided the foundation for the refinements in this second edition.

Preface to the Second Edition

In the seven years since the *Program Administration Scale* was first published, a growing body of research has emerged highlighting the importance of effective leadership and management practices in early childhood settings (Kagan, Kauerz, & Tarrant, 2008; Lower & Cassidy, 2007; Rohacek, Adams, & Kisker, 2010; Talan, 2007; Vu, Jeon, & Howes, 2008; Whitebook, Ryan, Kipnis, & Sakai, 2008). Several empirical studies have also been conducted that underscore the usefulness of the PAS as a reliable tool for measuring, monitoring, and improving administrative practices (Arend, 2010; Bloom & Talan, 2006; Kagan et al., 2008; McCormick Center for Early Childhood Leadership [MCECL], 2010a; McKelvey et al., 2010; Mietlicki, 2010; Miller & Bogatova, 2007; Rous et al., 2008).

Concurrently, the PAS has emerged as a useful tool in state quality rating and improvement systems (e.g., Illinois, Ohio, Arkansas, Montana), director credentialing initiatives (e.g., Tennessee, New Jersey), and in the self-study process for programs seeking accreditation by the National Association for the Education of Young Children (NAEYC) (Means & Pepper, 2010; Stephens, 2009). The rubrics for each indicator strand provide a convenient way for early childhood administrators to benchmark incremental change in the quality of their administrative practices.

While the research and anecdotal evidence from the field did not suggest the need for a major revision of the PAS, there was a need to share updated information supporting the reliability and validity of the instrument and to refine the wording of specific indicators.

To some degree, the second edition of the PAS has been "under construction" since it was first published in 2004. Practitioners using the PAS have asked probing questions about the indicators of administrative quality and provided insightful commentary about each of the PAS items. They have cast a bright light on how the PAS measures and supports best practice in a variety of program contexts. These practitioners, from across the country and representing all sectors of our field, have used the PAS for program self-improvement, research, training, college instruction, accreditation facilitation, quality monitoring, mentoring, coaching, organizational consulting, and policy making. Based on their feedback and new developments in the field, minor refinements have been made to support the reliable use of the PAS.

- A greater emphasis has been placed on administrative practices that support inclusion, cultural sensitivity, and linguistic diversity.

- Leadership routines and tools that provide opportunities for distributed leadership among staff have been included.

- The focus in technology now includes technological practices that promote effective communication, collaboration, and continuous learning.

- The definition for "Administrator" now aligns with NAEYC program accreditation criteria.

Finally, the Notes and Guiding Questions for the PAS items have been expanded in this second edition to increase understanding and facilitate greater consistency in completing the PAS by all users. Faculty at the McCormick Center for Early Childhood Leadership at National Louis University will continue to maintain updates and refinements to the PAS on the Center's website (McCormickCenter.nl.edu) and disseminate information about quality enhancement initiatives utilizing the tool.

Overview of the Program Administration Scale

Rationale

The genesis of the *Program Administration Scale* (PAS) was the growing professional consensus that early childhood program quality should be viewed through a broader lens than only the classroom learning environment. Without quality systems in place at the organizational level, high-quality interactions and learning environments at the classroom level cannot be sustained. While there were several instruments available to measure the quality of teacher-child interactions and the quality of the classroom instructional practices, until the development of the PAS there did not exist a valid and reliable instrument that solely measured the administrative practices of early childhood programs.

The instrument includes 25 items clustered in 10 subscales that measure both leadership and management functions of center-based early childhood programs. Leadership functions relate to the broad view of helping an organization clarify and affirm values, set goals, articulate a vision, and chart a course of action to achieve that vision. Management functions relate to the actual orchestration of tasks and the setting up of systems to carry out the organizational mission (Bloom, 2004).

Designed for early childhood program administrators, researchers, monitoring personnel, and quality enhancement facilitators, the PAS was constructed to complement the widely used classroom Environment Rating Scales developed by Harms, Clifford, and Cryer. Both the PAS and the Environment Rating Scales measure quality on a 7-point scale and both generate a profile to guide program improvement efforts. If used together, these instruments provide a focused look at best practices at the classroom level and the broad view of program quality from an organizational perspective (Kagan et al., 2008; McKelvey et al., 2010).

Multi-Use Design

The *Program Administration Scale* is applicable for multiple uses: program self-improvement, technical assistance and monitoring, training, research and evaluation, and public awareness. The target audience for the PAS is center-based early childhood programs, including Head Start and state-funded pre-K programs. The instrument is also appropriate for measuring and improving administrative quality in school-based early childhood programs.

- **Program self-improvement.** Because indicators are objective and quantifiable on a 7-point continuum from inadequate to excellent, center directors can easily set program goals to incrementally improve administrative practices. The resulting profile can be used to benchmark a center's progress in meeting those goals over time.

- **Technical assistance and monitoring.** As part of local or state quality enhancement initiatives, the PAS can serve as a convenient technical assistance and monitoring tool providing clear guidelines for incrementally improving organizational practices to ensure high-quality programming for children and families.

- **Training.** For both pre-service and in-service training for program administrators, the PAS provides a broad overview of organizational practices, highlights best practices in leadership and management, and reinforces the important role that program directors play in shaping program quality.

- **Research and evaluation.** For independent research studies or publicly funded quality rating and improvement systems (QRIS) that reward higher levels of program quality, the PAS can be used to describe current levels of program quality as well as benchmark change in pretest-posttest evaluation designs.

◆ **Public awareness.** Because the PAS is written in clear language and provides a rubric of concrete examples of different leadership and management practices, it can help inform a wide range of stakeholders—center directors, agency administrators, state policymakers, licensing representatives, teacher trainers, parents, and resource and referral specialists—about the components of high-quality programming.

Subscales, Items, and Indicators

As explained earlier, the PAS measures quality on a 7-point scale in 25 items clustered in 10 subscales. The first 23 items relate to all programs. The last two items (Item 24 Teacher and Item 25 Assistant Teacher/Aide) are optional items depending on the program's staffing pattern. Each item is comprised of 2 to 5 indicator strands, and each indicator strand is scored on a 7-point scale from inadequate to excellent.

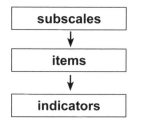

The following is a description of the subscales into which the items are grouped:

◆ **Human Resources Development** assesses whether the program provides an orientation for new staff, ongoing staff development, regular opportunities for supervision and support, and systematic performance appraisal.

◆ **Personnel Cost and Allocation** looks at whether the organization has a written salary scale and annual salary increases, the type and availability of fringe benefits, whether children are regrouped during the day to maintain ratios, and the availability of paid planning time for teaching staff.

◆ **Center Operations** considers the health and safety of the facility, whether the center has a risk-management plan, the adequacy of the space to meet the needs of staff, and the frequency and quality of internal communications, including shared leadership at staff meetings and conflict resolution.

◆ **Child Assessment** examines the availability of screening procedures to assist in the identification of children with special needs, the type and frequency of child assessments to determine learning and developmental outcomes, and whether the results of child assessments are used in lesson planning and program evaluation.

◆ **Fiscal Management** looks at the director's role in the annual budget planning process, if payroll and other expenses are paid in a timely manner, and if standard accounting procedures are adhered to.

◆ **Program Planning and Evaluation** assesses whether the center has a written mission and vision statement, engages in strategic planning, and involves staff and parents in evaluating program practices.

◆ **Family Partnerships** examines the type and frequency of communication with parents, their level of involvement in center activities and decision making, and the degree of support the center provides to parents from different cultural and linguistic backgrounds.

- **Marketing and Public Relations** evaluates the type and frequency of different external communication tools, how responsive the center is to the needs of the neighborhood or local community, and the administrator's involvement in early childhood professional organizations, as well as local civic, business, or faith-based organizations.

- **Technology** looks at the center's technological resources, how technology is used by administrative and teaching staff, and whether the center has clear policies and procedures regarding the appropriate use of technology at work and the confidentiality of work-related information.

- **Staff Qualifications** considers the level of general education, specialized training, and job experience of the Administrator and members of the teaching staff.

Definition of Terms

The following definitions are used consistently throughout the PAS and should be used in completing the PAS.

Administrative staff	Includes director, assistant director, and education coordinator.
Administrator	The individual who has primary responsibility for planning, implementing, and evaluating the early childhood program. The Administrator must be located on-site if the center has four or more classrooms or a total enrollment of 60 or more full-time equivalent (FTE) children. Role titles for the Administrator vary and may include director, manager, coordinator, or principal.
Assistant Teacher/Aide	A member of the teaching team assigned to a group of children who works under the direct supervision of the Lead Teacher and/or Teacher.
Center/Site	Unit of analysis for completing the PAS.
ECE/CD	Early childhood education or child development.
Lead Teacher	The individual with the highest professional qualifications assigned to teach a group of children and who is responsible for daily lesson planning, parent conferences, child assessment, and curriculum planning. This individual may also supervise other members of the teaching team. In some settings, this person is called a head teacher, master teacher, or teacher.
Parent	Includes parents and guardians.
sh	Semester hours of college credit.
Support staff	Includes kitchen, transportation, clerical, and maintenance staff.
Teacher	A member of the teaching team who shares responsibility with the Lead Teacher for the care and education of an assigned group of children.
Teaching staff	Includes Lead Teachers, Teachers, and Assistant Teachers/Aides.

Using the PAS

Data-Collection Procedures

The *Program Administration Scale* was designed for use by program administrators as well as by trained independent assessors such as researchers, consultants, and program evaluators. The independent assessor using the PAS should schedule approximately two hours for an interview with the Administrator and an additional two hours for a review of documents. In advance of the visit, it is recommended that the Administrator be provided with a copy of the PAS and the Documents for Review form, which is available on the McCormick Center's website (McCormickCenter.nl.edu).

Upon arriving for the interview, the assessor should first ask the Administrator for a brief tour of the facility, including the indoor and outdoor play environments, and any space specifically designated for families and staff. Observations of the facility are needed to complete the scoring of three items (Item 7 Facilities Management, Item 8 Risk Management, and Item 20 Technological Resources). For the indicators needing documentation, the assessor should record a preliminary rating based on statements made by the Administrator during the interview. After the interview, a thorough review of the documents should be conducted and adjustments made to the rating of the indicators if necessary.

For Items 1–21, Guiding Questions are provided to assist in rating the indicators. These questions can be found on the page preceding the scoring page for each item. Center directors should use these questions as prompts for rating the indicators. Independent assessors may find the questions useful to elicit information from the Administrator during the interview.

Scoring the PAS

Adhering to the following two scoring principles for the *Program Administration Scale* will ensure the accuracy of the PAS profile and promote consistency in scoring across programs.

- In order to provide an accurate snapshot of program administrative practices, it is important that ratings be based only on the indicators provided for each item. For some indicators, scores are based solely on the Administrator's self-report (e.g., Item 6 Staffing Patterns and Scheduling, Indicator 3.1). However, for most indicators, it is necessary to review documents or make observations in order to verify the accuracy of the information provided by the Administrator. For these verifiable indicators, a "D" (document) or an "O" (observation) appears under the indicator number (e.g., Item 6 Staffing Patterns and Scheduling, Indicator 5.1).

- Scores should be based on existing policies and procedures, not past practices or plans for the future.

The following protocol should be used to score the *Program Administration Scale*:

Step 1. Rate the indicators for Items 1–21.
Use the following rules for rating the indicators:

- For each item, begin with the indicators under the 1 (inadequate) category and proceed across the continuum of quality for each indicator to 7 (excellent), writing in the spaces provided a Y (yes) or N (no) if each indicator applies.

- A rating of N/A (not applicable) may be given for indicators or for entire items when "N/A is allowed" is shown on the scale. Indicators rated N/A are not counted when determining the score for an item, and items scored N/A are not counted when calculating the Total PAS Score.

- Record notes or supporting evidence for each indicator in the empty space on each page (e.g., practice described meets the criteria specified or an observation is made).

- After rating all indicators for Items 1–21 and verifying documentation, record the rationale for any indicators where credit is not received in the space labeled *Rationale* at the bottom of each scale page.

Step 2. Determine the scores for Items 1–21.

Use the following scoring rules for determining the item scores:

- A score of 1 is given if any indicator under the 1 column is rated Y (yes). A score of 1 is also given if all indicators under the 1 column are rated N (no) and less than half of the indicators under the 3 column are rated Y (yes).

- A score of 2 is given when all indicators under 1 are rated N (no) and at least half of the indicators under 3 are rated Y (yes).

- A score of 3 is given when all indicators under 1 are rated N (no) and all indicators under 3 are rated Y (yes).

- A score of 4 is given when all indicators under 1 are rated N (no), all indicators under 3 are rated Y (yes), and at least half of the indicators under 5 are rated Y (yes).

- A score of 5 is given when all indicators under 1 are rated N (no) and all indicators under 3 and 5 are rated Y (yes).

- A score of 6 is given when all indicators under 1 are rated N (no), all the indicators under 3 and 5 are rated Y (yes), and at least half of the indicators under 7 are rated Y (yes).

- A score of 7 is given when all indicators under 1 are rated N (no) and all indicators under 3, 5, and 7 are rated Y (yes).

Circle the item score in the space provided in the lower right-hand corner on each item page.

Step 3. Determine the scores for Items 22–25.

Complete the **Administrator Qualifications Worksheet** (page 62). Only one person is designated as the Administrator.

- Use this information to rate the indicators for Item 22 Administrator.

- Follow the scoring rules provided in Steps 1 and 2.

Complete a **Teaching Staff Qualifications Worksheet** (page 63) for each group of children, duplicating the form as needed.

- For completing the PAS, it is necessary to designate one of the adults responsible for the care and education of an assigned group of children as the Lead Teacher. The Lead Teacher is the individual with the highest professional qualifications. If there are co-teachers, the Lead Teacher is the individual with the highest professional qualifications.

- Designate any other member of the teaching team who shares responsibility with the Lead Teacher for the care and education of an assigned group of children as a Teacher.

- Designate any member of the teaching team who works under the direct supervision of the Lead Teacher and/or Teacher as an Assistant Teacher/Aide.

- Not all centers will have a staffing pattern that includes Teachers and/or Assistant Teachers/Aides.

- Use the information from the **Teaching Staff Qualifications Worksheet** to rate the indicators for Item 23 Lead Teacher, Item 24 Teacher, and Item 25 Assistant Teacher/Aide.

- Duplicate sufficient copies of Items 23, 24, and 25 so that the qualifications of each member of the teaching staff can be rated separately.

- Follow the rules provided in Steps 1 and 2 to score the teaching staff qualification Items 23, 24, and 25.

Complete the **Summary of Teaching Staff Qualifications Worksheet** (page 64).

- Transfer the individual item scores for each member of the teaching staff to the **Summary of Teaching Staff Qualifications Worksheet**.

- Use the qualifications of the Lead Teachers assigned to each group of children to compute the Item 23 Average Score. Round this score to the closest whole number and enter on the **Item Summary** form (page 65) for Item 23.

- Use the qualifications of any Teachers assigned to each group of children to compute the Item 24 Average Score. Round this score to the closest whole number and enter on the **Item Summary** form for Item 24.

- Use the qualifications of any Assistant Teachers/Aides assigned to each group of children to compute the Item 25 Average Score. Round this score to the closest whole number and enter on the **Item Summary** form for Item 25.

Step 4. Generate a Total PAS Score.

The Total PAS Score is the sum of the item scores. To calculate this score, transfer the individual item scores to the **Item Summary** form on page 65. Sum the item scores for the entire scale.

- If the program has a staffing pattern that includes Teachers **and** Assistant Teachers/Aides, then 25 items are rated and the possible range of scores is 25–175.

- If the program has a staffing pattern that includes Teachers **or** Assistant Teachers/Aides, then 24 items are rated and the possible range of scores is 24–168.

- If the program has a staffing pattern that does not include Teachers **or** Assistant Teachers/Aides, then 23 items are scored and the possible range of scores is 23–161.

Step 5. Determine the Average PAS Item Score.

Use the **Item Summary** form to calculate the Average PAS Item Score, which is the Total PAS Score divided by the number of items scored (a minimum of 23 for all programs; 24 or 25 for programs that have a staffing pattern that includes Teachers and/or Assistant Teachers/Aides).

Step 6. Plot scores on the PAS Profile.

Plot the individual item scores on the graph of the **PAS Profile** on page 66; then connect the dots. Add the information at the bottom of the profile regarding the Total PAS Score, number of items scored, and Average PAS Item Score.

Item Summary

Program: _Anywhere Child Care Center_   Date: _3/7/11_

Instructions

Use this form to summarize the item scores and to calculate the Total PAS Score and Average PAS Item Score.

- Enter the item scores in the spaces provided.
- Sum all the item scores and enter the total in the space provided. This is the Total PAS Score.
- Divide the Total PAS Score by the total number of items (minimum of 23 for all programs; 24 or 25 for programs that have a staffing pattern that includes Teachers and/or Assistant Teachers/Aides). The resulting number is the Average PAS Item Score.

Item	Score
1. Staff Orientation	3
2. Supervision and Performance Appraisal	5
3. Staff Development	4
4. Compensation	4
5. Benefits	6
6. Staffing Patterns and Scheduling	2
7. Facilities Management	4
8. Risk Management	4
9. Internal Communications	5
10. Screening and Identification of Special Needs	6
11. Assessment in Support of Learning	5
12. Budget Planning	4
13. Accounting Practices	5
14. Program Evaluation	6
15. Strategic Planning	3
16. Family Communications	5
17. Family Support and Involvement	6
18. External Communications	3
19. Community Outreach	4
20. Technological Resources	3
21. Use of Technology	3
22. Administrator	3
23. Lead Teacher	4
24. Teacher (N/A is allowed)	NA
25. Assistant Teacher/Aide (N/A is allowed)	2

Sum of item scores

99	÷	24	=	4.13
Total PAS Score		Number of items scored		Average PAS Item Score

65

The Program Administration Scale Profile

Program: _Anywhere Child Care Center_   Date: _3/7/11_

Subscales	Items	1	2	3	4	5	6	7
Human Resources Development	1. Staff Orientation							
	2. Supervision and Performance Appraisal							
	3. Staff Development							
Personnel Cost and Allocation	4. Compensation							
	5. Benefits							
	6. Staffing Patterns and Scheduling							
Center Operations	7. Facilities Management							
	8. Risk Management							
	9. Internal Communications							
Child Assessment	10. Screening and Identification of Special Needs							
	11. Assessment in Support of Learning							
Fiscal Management	12. Budget Planning							
	13. Accounting Practices							
Program Planning and Evaluation	14. Program Evaluation							
	15. Strategic Planning							
Family Partnerships	16. Family Communications							
	17. Family Support and Involvement							
Marketing and Public Relations	18. External Communications							
	19. Community Outreach							
Technology	20. Technological Resources							
	21. Use of Technology							
Staff Qualifications	22. Administrator							
	23. Lead Teacher							
	24. Teacher (N/A is allowed)							
	25. Assistant Teacher/Aide (N/A is allowed)							

Total PAS Score _99_   ÷ Number of items _24_   = Average PAS Item Score _4.13_

66

Program Administration Scale

Subscales and Items

Human Resources Development

1. Staff Orientation
2. Supervision and Performance Appraisal
3. Staff Development

Personnel Cost and Allocation

4. Compensation
5. Benefits
6. Staffing Patterns and Scheduling

Center Operations

7. Facilities Management
8. Risk Management
9. Internal Communications

Child Assessment

10. Screening and Identification of Special Needs
11. Assessment in Support of Learning

Fiscal Management

12. Budget Planning
13. Accounting Practices

Program Planning and Evaluation

14. Program Evaluation
15. Strategic Planning

Family Partnerships

16. Family Communications
17. Family Support and Involvement

Marketing and Public Relations

18. External Communications
19. Community Outreach

Technology

20. Technological Resources
21. Use of Technology

Staff Qualifications

22. Administrator
23. Lead Teacher
24. Teacher
25. Assistant Teacher/Aide

Human Resources Development

1. Staff Orientation

Notes	Guiding Questions

*   Written orientation procedures **must** be specific to the early childhood program but may also include the orientation procedures of a sponsoring agency.
 	
   The written orientation procedures **must** include:
    ❏ a timeframe for the orientation process
    ❏ activities to occur during the orientation process
    ❏ personnel involved in the orientation process
    ❏ specific employment forms required
    ❏ specific written policies and procedures to be provided to new staff
 	
**   A system to ensure that staff orientation is consistently implemented **must** include:
    ❏ tangible, concrete evidence
    ❏ involvement of multiple individuals
    ❏ a defined process of accountability
 	
***   The purpose of this feedback is to provide newly hired staff the opportunity to improve the orientation process for future employees.
	What happens when new staff are hired?
	  • Is there an orientation? What does it include?
	  • What written materials do new staff receive?
	  • Is there an introductory/probationary period with feedback provided by a supervisor?
	  • Before assuming their job responsibilities, do new teaching staff meet children and co-workers?
	  • As part of the orientation process, do new teaching staff observe in their assigned classrooms/groups before assuming their job responsibilities?
	
	Are there written orientation procedures?
	  • What do they include?
	  • Are they reviewed? How often?
	
	Is orientation implemented consistently for new staff?
	  • Is there a system for ensuring that orientation is consistently implemented?
	  • What happens at the end of orientation? Do new staff provide feedback about the orientation process?

Human Resources Development

1. Staff Orientation

1	2	3	4	5	6	7
Inadequate		Minimal		Good		Excellent

___ 1.1 There is no orientation for new staff.

___ 3.1 D includes receiving the job description, employee handbook, parent handbook, and personnel policies.

___ 5.1 D The orientation includes feedback from the supervisor during the introductory or probationary period.

___ 7.1 D The orientation for new teaching staff includes observation in the assigned classroom and meeting children and co-workers prior to assuming responsibilities.

___ 1.2 There are no written orientation procedures.

___ 3.2 D There are written orientation procedures.*

___ 5.2 D The written orientation procedures have been reviewed within the last three years.*

___ 7.2 D The written orientation procedures are reviewed annually.*

___ 1.3 Staff orientation is not consistently implemented.

___ 3.3 Staff orientation is consistently implemented.

___ 5.3 D There is a system to ensure that staff orientation is consistently implemented.**

___ 7.3 D Written feedback about the orientation process is obtained from newly hired staff at the conclusion of the introductory or probationary period.***

Rationale:

Circle the final score based on the scoring rules on pages 4–5.

1   2   3   4   5   6   7

1. Staff Orientation

2. Supervision and Performance Appraisal

Notes	Guiding Questions
This item is concerned with the supervision and performance appraisal of teaching staff only. * Written goals for professional development **must** relate to the performance appraisal criteria and specify desired improvements in professional practice. *Professional development activities* refers to the specific professional development strategies (e.g., college course, online training, workshop, observation by a mentor, observation of another teacher/classroom) planned to achieve identified goals. ** Teaching staff are formally observed when the observation is conducted for the exclusive purpose of assessing and improving teaching practices. *** A system to provide ongoing feedback and support to teaching staff **must** include: ❒ tangible, concrete evidence ❒ involvement of multiple individuals ❒ a defined process of accountability	How are teaching staff evaluated? • How often do performance appraisals occur? • Who participates? How are they involved? • Does the performance appraisal include setting goals relating to performance appraisal criteria? • Does the performance appraisal include specific development strategies? What type of criteria are used to evaluate performance? • Are criteria mostly subjective or objective? • Are criteria tied to the specific responsibilities detailed in each job description? • Are there other other sources of evidence considered in the performance appraisal process? How is supervision provided for teaching staff? • Are teaching staff formally observed? How often? • Are teaching staff provided with feedback based on a formal observation? How often? • Is there a system to ensure that teaching staff are provided with ongoing feedback and support?

2. Supervision and Performance Appraisal

1	2	3	4	5	6	7
Inadequate		**Minimal**		**Good**		**Excellent**

___ 1.1 Written annual performance appraisal is not conducted by the supervisor for all teaching staff (Lead Teachers, Teachers, and/or Assistant Teachers/Aides).

___ 3.1 D Written annual performance appraisal is conducted by the supervisor for all teaching staff (Lead Teachers, Teachers, and/or Assistant Teachers/Aides).

___ 5.1 D All teaching staff (Lead Teachers, Teachers, and/or Assistant Teachers/Aides) participate in an annual performance appraisal process (e.g., written self-appraisal).

___ 7.1 D Written annual performance appraisal for all teaching staff (Lead Teachers, Teachers, and/or Assistant Teachers/ Aides) includes goals and professional development activities for the next year.*

___ 1.2 Criteria used for performance appraisal are mostly subjective and trait-based (e.g., teacher is warm, friendly, caring).

___ 3.2 D Criteria used for performance appraisal are mostly objective and behavior-based (e.g., teacher uses positive guidance techniques, asks children open-ended questions).

___ 5.2 D Criteria used for performance appraisal differ by role and are tied to the specific responsibilities detailed in each job description.

___ 7.2 D The performance appraisal process includes multiple sources of evidence (e.g., artifacts, parent feedback, co-worker feedback).

___ 1.3 Teaching staff are not formally observed as part of the supervision and performance appraisal process.**

___ 3.3 Teaching staff are formally observed as part of the supervision and performance appraisal process.**

___ 5.3 D At least three times a year, supervisors provide teaching staff with written or verbal feedback based on formal observation of performance.**

___ 7.3 D A system is implemented to provide ongoing feedback and support to all teaching staff.***

Rationale:

Circle the final score based on the scoring rules on pages 4–5.

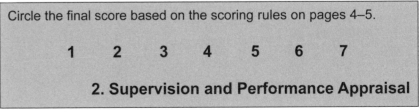

1	2	3	4	5	6	7

2. Supervision and Performance Appraisal

3. Staff Development

Notes	Guiding Questions

* An individualized model of staff development **must** include:
   ❏ an individual's specific training needs
   ❏ an action plan to meet those needs
 	
** A system to support the career development of teaching and administrative staff **must** include:
   ❏ tangible, concrete evidence
   ❏ involvement of multiple individuals
   ❏ a defined process of accountability
	Is staff development provided on-site or paid for off-site?
	  • For whom is staff development provided?
	  • Is job-specific staff development provided? For whom?
	
	Does the center have a policy regarding staff development?
	  • What is the minimum number of staff development hours required by the center?
	  • What is the process to keep track of staff development hours?
	  • Is staff development tailored to meet individual staff member needs? How is this accomplished?
	
	What publicly-funded professional development opportunities are available for staff?
	  • How do staff find out about these opportunities?
	  • Is there a system to support the career development of staff?

14

3. Staff Development

1	2	3	4	5	6	7
Inadequate		**Minimal**		**Good**		**Excellent**

___ 1.1 No provision is made for staff development.

___ 3.1 Staff development for all
D teaching staff is provided on-site or paid for off-site.

___ 5.1 Staff development for all
D teaching, support, and administrative staff is provided on-site or paid for off-site.

___ 7.1 Job-specific staff development
D is provided (e.g., administrators receive training on budgeting; teachers receive training on positive guidance).

___ 1.2 The program does not have a policy requiring all teaching and administrative staff to attend 15 or more clock hours of staff development each year **and** a training log is not maintained.

___ 3.2 The program has a policy
D requiring all teaching and administrative staff to attend 15 or more clock hours of staff development each year **and** a training log is maintained.

___ 5.2 The program has a policy
D requiring all teaching and administrative staff to attend 20 or more clock hours of staff development each year **and** a training log is maintained.

___ 7.2 An individualized model of
D staff development is utilized for teaching and administrative staff.*

___ 1.3 The Administrator is not familiar with publicly funded professional development opportunities available to staff (e.g., workshops, scholarships, wage enhancement initiatives).

___ 3.3 The Administrator is familiar with publicly funded professional development opportunities available to staff (e.g., workshops, scholarships, wage enhancement initiatives).

___ 5.3 Information regarding
D publicly funded professional development opportunities is posted and/or communicated to staff on an ongoing basis.

___ 7.3 A system exists to support
D the career development of teaching and administrative staff (e.g., regularly scheduled time to meet with a supervisor or mentor to monitor progress toward career goals).**

Rationale:

Circle the final score based on the scoring rules on pages 4–5.

1 2 3 4 5 6 7

3. Staff Development

Personnel Cost and Allocation

4. Compensation

Notes	Guiding Questions
* *Available* means unrestricted access to the written salary scale identifying the beginning salary/wage for new employees based on predetermined criteria. ** *Internal equity* refers to the relationship between different jobs within an organization and is achieved through job analysis to determine the relative value or contribution of the work to the organization's goals. *External equity* refers to the relationship between similar jobs in the external labor market and is achieved by establishing the going rate for similar work performed by employees with similar qualifications. *** *Education* refers to the level of general education (e.g., high school diploma, associate's degree, bachelor's degree). *Specialized training* refers to college coursework or other training specific to the role. *Professional credentials* refers to the certificates/licenses issued to early childhood practitioners by state agencies or national organizations in recognition of the achievement of professional competency.	Is there a written salary scale? • Who has access to the salary scale? • How often is it reviewed? For what purpose? What criteria is the salary scale based on? • Is it based on different roles? • Is it based on different levels of education and specialized training? • Is it based on years of relevant experience? • Is it based on professional credentials? What types of salary increases are available to employees? • When was the last time employees received a salary increase? • Were all employees eligible? • Did employees receive an annual increase in each of the last three years? Were all employees eligible? • Do employees receive merit increases in addition to annual salary increases?

Personnel Cost and Allocation

4. Compensation

1	2	3	4	5	6	7
Inadequate		**Minimal**		**Good**		**Excellent**

___ 1.1 A written salary scale is not available.*

___ 3.1 D A written salary scale is available to some center employees.*

___ 5.1 D A written salary scale is available to all center employees.*

___ 7.1 D The written salary scale was reviewed at least twice within the last five years for internal and external equity.**

___ 1.2 A written salary scale is based only on role.

___ 3.2 D A written salary scale is differentiated by role, education, and specialized training.***

___ 5.2 D A written salary scale is differentiated by role, education, specialized training, and years of relevant experience.***

___ 7.2 D A written salary scale is differentiated by role, education, specialized training, years of relevant experience, and professional credentials.***

___ 1.3 All employees (administrative, teaching, and support staff) did not receive a salary increase within the last two years.

___ 3.3 D All employees (administrative, teaching, and support staff) received a salary increase within the last two years.

___ 5.3 D All employees (administrative, teaching, and support staff) received an annual salary increase in each of the last three years.

___ 7.3 D The center has a compensation plan that provides for merit increases in addition to annual salary increases.

Rationale:

Circle the final score based on the scoring rules on pages 4–5.

1	2	3	4	5	6	7

4. Compensation

5. Benefits

Notes	Guiding Questions
Employment terms:	What health benefits are available to all full-time employees?
	• Does the organization pay a percentage of the employee's premium?
All full-time employees refers to paid employees who work 35 or more hours per week unless the organization defines full-time employment differently as noted in the personnel policies or employee handbook.	What sick/personal day benefits are available to all employees?
	• Are they available during the first year of employment?
All employees refers to full-time and part-time paid employees who work 20 or more hours per week. Work-study, seasonal, and part-time employees who work less than 20 hours per week are not included.	What paid vacation benefits are available to all employees?
	• Are they available during the first year of employment?
	• Does this benefit increase over time?
* N/A is allowed only if there are no full-time employees.	What retirement benefits are available to all full-time employees?
	• Does the organization match a portion of the employee's salary contributed to a retirement plan?
** Vacation days are days of paid time off that are in addition to a minimum of 6 paid holidays that are commonly observed by the program.	What professional development benefits are available to all employees?
	• Is there a specific dollar amount identified?
*** The professional development benefit gives employees financial support to access professional development of their own choosing. Supervisor approval may be required.	

5. Benefits

	1	2	3	4	5	6	7
	Inadequate		Minimal		Good		Excellent

___ 1.1 All full-time employees do not have the option to purchase health insurance with the employer paying a portion of the cost (N/A is allowed).*

___ 3.1 D All full-time employees have the option to purchase health insurance with the employer paying a portion of the cost (N/A is allowed).*

___ 5.1 D All full-time employees have the option to purchase health insurance with the employer paying 50% or more of the cost of the employee's coverage (N/A is allowed).*

___ 7.1 D All full-time employees have the option to purchase health insurance with the employer paying 66% or more of the cost of the employee's coverage (N/A is allowed).*

___ 1.2 All employees do not receive at least 6 paid sick/personal days during their first year of employment.

___ 3.2 D All employees receive 6 or more paid sick/personal days during their first year of employment.

___ 5.2 D All employees receive 9 or more paid sick/personal days during their first year of employment.

___ 7.2 D All employees receive 12 or more paid sick/personal days during their first year of employment.

___ 1.3 All employees do not receive at least 5 paid vacation days during the first year of employment.**

___ 3.3 D All employees receive 5 or more paid vacation days during the first year of employment.**

___ 5.3 D All employees receive 10 or more paid vacation days during the second and third years of employment.**

___ 7.3 D All employees receive 15 or more paid vacation days during the fourth year of employment.**

___ 1.4 All full-time employees do not have the option of contributing to a retirement plan (N/A is allowed).*

___ 3.4 D All full-time employees have the option of contributing to a retirement plan (N/A is allowed).*

___ 5.4 D The employer matches 3% or more of the employee's salary contributed to a retirement plan (N/A is allowed).*

___ 7.4 D The employer matches 5% or more of the employee's salary contributed to a retirement plan (N/A is allowed).*

___ 1.5 The employer does not make any provision to pay for or reimburse professional development expenses.***

___ 3.5 D The employer makes some provision to pay for or reimburse professional development expenses.***

___ 5.5 D The employer provides $100 or more per year to all employees to pay for or reimburse professional development expenses.***

___ 7.5 D The employer provides $200 or more per year to all employees to pay for or reimburse professional development expenses.***

Rationale:

Circle the final score based on the scoring rules on pages 4–5.

1   2   3   4   5   6   7

5. Benefits

6. Staffing Patterns and Scheduling

Notes	Guiding Questions
* *Regrouped to maintain required ratios* refers to when children are moved from one group to another because a member of the teaching team is absent, resulting in noncompliance with the required teacher-child ratio. ** *Regrouped at the beginning or end of the day* refers to an intentional and consistent regrouping of children when a reduced number of children is present. *** Paid planning and preparation time can occur during the children's naptime as long as it does not interfere with the adequate supervision of children.	How often are children regrouped to maintain required ratios? • Are there regularly scheduled times when children are regrouped to maintain required ratios? When does this occur? • How is classroom coverage ensured when a member of the teaching staff is absent? Are members of the teaching staff given paid planning and preparation time? • How often does it occur? For how long? • Where does it take place? Are children present? • Do teaching staff collaborate on curriculum planning? How often? Who is involved? What is considered in developing the staffing schedule? • Does the staffing schedule allow for a staff member to be alone in the center with a child? • Does the staffing schedule allow for a staff member to be alone with a child in a classroom? If so, when and for how long? How often does the Administrator spend time in the classroom to maintain required ratios?

6. Staffing Patterns and Scheduling

1	2	3	4	5	6	7
Inadequate		**Minimal**		**Good**		**Excellent**

___ 1.1 Children are regrouped to maintain required ratios six or more times per year.*

    ___ 3.1 Children are regrouped to maintain required ratios less than six times per year.*

    ___ 5.1 D The staffing plan anticipates absences of teaching staff by providing "staffing over ratio" or a "floating teacher."

    ___ 7.1 D The staffing plan provides classroom coverage so that children are not regrouped at the beginning or end of the day.**

___ 1.2 There is no regularly scheduled paid planning or preparation time for teaching staff.***

    ___ 3.2 D There is regularly scheduled paid planning or preparation time for teaching staff.***

    ___ 5.2 D Paid curriculum planning time occurs at least every other week and includes all teaching staff working with the same group of children.

    ___ 7.2 D Teaching staff have the equivalent of at least 30 minutes of paid planning or preparation time per day that does not occur in the presence of children.

___ 1.3 In the center, two or more staff are not scheduled whenever children are present.

    ___ 3.3 D In the center, two or more staff are scheduled whenever children are present.

    ___ 5.3 D In each classroom, two or more teaching staff are scheduled whenever children are present (exception allowed during the first and last hour of operation).

    ___ 7.3 D In each classroom, two or more teaching staff are scheduled whenever children are present (including the first and last hour of operation).

___ 1.4 The Administrator spends time in a classroom to maintain required ratios more than once a week (N/A is allowed for programs with less than 60 children).

    ___ 3.4 The Administrator spends time in a classroom to maintain required ratios no more than once a week (N/A is allowed for programs with less than 60 children).

    ___ 5.4 The Administrator spends time in a classroom to maintain required ratios no more than once a month (N/A is allowed for programs with less than 60 children).

    ___ 7.4 The Administrator spends time in a classroom to maintain required ratios no more than four times per year (N/A is allowed for programs with less than 60 children).

Rationale:

Circle the final score based on the scoring rules on pages 4–5.

1	2	3	4	5	6	7

6. Staffing Patterns and Scheduling

Center Operations

7. Facilities Management

Notes	Guiding Questions

* *Safe appearance* means that the overall impression is that the facility, equipment, and outdoor environment are clean and well-maintained.
 	
** Examples of routine maintenance **may** include:
  ❏ contract for cleaning services
  ❏ contract for maintenance of the heating or cooling system
  ❏ record of maintenance of playground equipment, fire extinguisher, or alarm system
  ❏ other_____
 	
*** A system of routine maintenance **must** include:
  ❏ tangible, concrete evidence
  ❏ involvement of multiple individuals
  ❏ a defined process of accountability
 	
**** Space that meets the needs of staff **must** include:
  ❏ a separate adult restroom
  ❏ an enclosed storage area for personal belongings
  ❏ an adult-sized chair or sofa in each classroom
 	
***** A professional library **must** include:
  ❏ a minimum of 25 books related to early childhood education
  ❏ a minimum of 12 issues of a journal/magazine related to early childhood education
	What are some examples of routine maintenance for the facility?
	  • Is there a system to ensure that routine maintenance happens as planned?
	
	How does the space meet the needs of staff?
	  • What facilities, equipment, furniture, and materials are provided for staff?
	
	Is there administrative office space?
	  • Where is it located?
	  • Is there office space on-site for private meetings?
	  • How is the office space equipped?

Center Operations

7. Facilities Management

1	2	3	4	5	6	7
Inadequate		**Minimal**		**Good**		**Excellent**

___ 1.1 The facility and/or outdoor play environment appear unsafe.*

___ 3.1 O The facility and outdoor play environment appear safe.*

___ 5.1 D There are at least two examples of routine maintenance for the facility.**

___ 7.1 D There is a system of routine maintenance for the facility.***

___ 1.2 Space is not provided for meeting the needs of staff.****

___ 3.2 O Space is provided for meeting the needs of staff.****

___ 5.2 O Space with adult-sized furniture is provided for staff use during breaks, meetings, conferences, and preparation time (dual use of space is allowed).

___ 7.2 O There is dedicated space for staff use only and staff have access to a professional library on-site.*****

___ 1.3 Administrative office space is not available on-site.

___ 3.3 O Administrative office space is available on-site and is equipped with an adult-sized desk or work station, an adult-sized chair, and file storage.

___ 5.3 O Separate administrative office space is available on-site allowing for private conversations and meetings.

___ 7.3 O Administrative office space is equipped with computer, printer, Internet access, fax/scanner and photocopying capacity, and answering machine or telephone with voicemail.

Rationale:

Circle the final score based on the scoring rules on pages 4–5.

1   2   3   4   5   6   7

7. Facilities Management

8. Risk Management

Notes	Guiding Questions
* The center's risk management plan **must** include: ☐ clear procedures to follow in the event of an emergency (e.g., fire, severe storm, intruder, accident) ☐ clear procedures to reduce the risk of allegations of child abuse or neglect (e.g., an open door policy for families, consistent use of accident reports, daily sign-in and sign-out by families) ☐ clear procedures to maintain the safety of people, facilities, equipment, and/or materials (e.g., universal precautions, sanitizing toys, servicing the fire extinguisher or alarm system). ** A system to ensure that emergency medical information is available to all teaching staff and substitutes **must** include: ☐ tangible, concrete evidence ☐ involvement of multiple individuals ☐ a defined process of accountability *** A system to ensure that emergency drills occur as planned **must** include: ☐ tangible, concrete evidence ☐ involvement of multiple individuals ☐ a defined process of accountability	Does the center have a written risk management plan? • What does the risk management plan include? • Where is it located? • How often is the plan reviewed? How is information about children's allergies and chronic medical conditions documented? • Where is information on children's allergies and chronic medical conditions kept? • How is the information communicated to staff? • How is the information communicated to substitutes? What types of emergency drills are practiced? • How often is each type of drill practiced? • How are the drills evaluated? • Is there a system to ensure that drills happen as planned? How are staff prepared to respond to medical emergencies? • How many staff are certified in CPR and First Aid? • When are certified staff required to be present? • How frequently is certification training provided?

8. Risk Management

1	2	3	4	5	6	7
Inadequate		**Minimal**		**Good**		**Excellent**

___ 1.1 No written risk management plan is available.

___ 3.1 D A written risk management plan is available.*

___ 5.1 O A written risk management plan is available in each classroom.*

___ 7.1 D The written risk management plan is reviewed annually.*

___ 1.2 Information on individual children's allergies is not posted in the classroom **and** information about children's chronic medical conditions is not kept in the office files.

___ 3.2 O Information on individual children's allergies is posted in the classroom **and** information about children's chronic medical conditions is kept in the office files.

___ 5.2 O Information about individual children's chronic medical conditions is kept in the children's classrooms as well as in the office files.

___ 7.2 D A system is in place to ensure that necessary medical information is available to all teaching staff (including substitute teachers).**

___ 1.3 During the past year, fire drills were not practiced once a month.

___ 3.3 D During the past year, fire drills were practiced once a month **and** indoor emergency drills (e.g., severe storms, intruder) were practiced twice a year.

___ 5.3 D The fire and indoor emergency drill records include improvements needed.

___ 7.3 D A system is in place to ensure that emergency drills occur as planned.***

___ 1.4 The center does not have at least one staff person certified in CPR and First Aid on-site during all hours of operation.

___ 3.4 The center has at least one staff person certified in CPR and First Aid on-site during all hours of operation.

___ 5.4 D The center has at least one staff person certified in CPR and First Aid assigned in each classroom.

___ 7.4 D The center annually provides certification training on CPR and First Aid for staff.

Rationale:

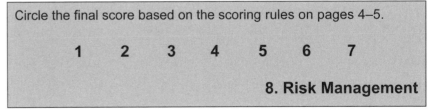

Circle the final score based on the scoring rules on pages 4–5.

1   2   3   4   5   6   7

8. Risk Management

9. Internal Communications

Notes	Questions
* Examples of different modes of internal communication **may** include: ❐ face-to-face conversation ❐ in-house newsletters ❐ internal memos ❐ e-mail ❐ staff bulletin board ❐ voicemail ❐ text messaging ❐ message book ❐ routing slips ❐ other_____ ** *Minutes* refers to written records of what occurs at staff meetings. *** A conflict resolution policy is more than a statement describing who to go to with a grievance. The policy **must** address conflict resolution in the context of the work environment and identify an expectation that staff work together to resolve their disputes using open, professional communication.	What methods are used at the center to communicate information to staff? Are there regularly scheduled staff meetings? • How frequently do scheduled centerwide meetings occur? • How frequently do scheduled team meetings occur? Who is involved in planning centerwide staff meetings? Who is involved in facilitating discussions at centerwide staff meetings? Are minutes of staff meetings maintained? • What do the minutes contain? • How are the minutes used? • When are they available for staff to review? How are staff disputes resolved? • Is there a written policy regarding the handling of staff disputes? What does it include? • Is training provided for staff on conflict resolution? • Are there clear written procedures to guide staff in implementing the conflict resolution policy?

9. Internal Communications

1	2	3	4	5	6	7
Inadequate		**Minimal**		**Good**		**Excellent**

___ 1.1 Information is communicated only verbally.

___ 1.2 There are not at least two regularly scheduled, centerwide staff meetings per year.

___ 1.3 Staff are not involved in planning centerwide staff meetings.

___ 1.4 Minutes are not kept of topics discussed and decisions made at staff meetings.**

___ 1.5 There is no written conflict resolution policy regarding the handling of staff disputes.***

___ 3.1 D Information is communicated in two or more ways.*

___ 3.2 D There are at least two regularly scheduled, centerwide staff meetings per year.

___ 3.3 D Staff are involved in planning centerwide staff meetings.

___ 3.4 D Minutes are kept of topics discussed and decisions made at staff meetings.**

___ 3.5 D There is a written conflict resolution policy regarding the handling of staff disputes.***

___ 5.1 D Information is communicated in four or more ways.*

___ 5.2 D There are regularly scheduled staff meetings that occur at least once a month (may include team or centerwide meetings).

___ 5.3 D Teaching staff occasionally lead the discussion of agenda items during centerwide staff meetings.

___ 5.4 D Minutes reflect an action plan for decisions made (e.g., activities, timeline, who is accountable).**

___ 5.5 D Training in conflict resolution was provided for staff within the past year.

___ 7.1 D Information is communicated in six or more ways.*

___ 7.2 D There are regularly scheduled staff meetings that occur at least twice a month (may include team or centerwide meetings).

___ 7.3 D Teaching staff consistently lead the discussion of agenda items during centerwide staff meetings.

___ 7.4 D Minutes are distributed in advance of staff meetings and action plans revisited at subsequent meetings.**

___ 7.5 D There are written procedures to guide staff implementation of a conflict resolution policy (behavior or communication strategies to be used).***

Rationale:

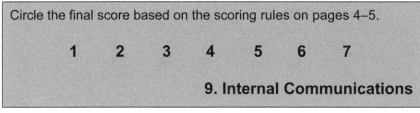

Circle the final score based on the scoring rules on pages 4–5.

1   2   3   4   5   6   7

9. Internal Communications

Child Assessment

10. Screening and Identification of Special Needs

Notes	Guiding Questions
* *Screening* refers to the first step in a two-step process to identify children with potential challenges in learning or development. Screening tools are administered to determine if a referral for further evaluation is necessary.	Are children screened for the purpose of identifying possible special needs? • How are children selected for screening? • What screening tool is used? Does it have established reliability and validity? • What safeguards are used to protect against the misidentification of children?
** Safeguards **must** include: ❏ screenings are conducted and interpreted by qualified professionals ❏ multiple sources of evidence are used (e.g., parent and/or staff input based on home and center observations) ❏ children are screened in their primary language	Are parents involved in the screening and identification process? • How are they notified before the screening? • How are they informed of screening results? • How are they involved in any plans for children resulting from the screening process?
*** A *special plan* refers to adaptations made by the teaching staff regarding classroom routines, activities, or daily schedule.	What happens if children are identified in the screening process as having a possible special need? • How does the center collaborate with specialists working with children with special needs? • Is there a system to support collaboration with specialists working with children with special needs?
**** A system to support collaboration with specialists **must** include: ❏ tangible, concrete evidence ❏ involvement of multiple individuals ❏ a defined process of accountability	
The required elements of a system to support collaboration with specialists are met if there is an Individualized Education Plan (IEP) or an Individualized Family Service Plan (IFSP) which includes the Administrator and/or a staff member from the center.	

Child Assessment

10. Screening and Identification of Special Needs

1	2	3	4	5	6	7
Inadequate		**Minimal**		**Good**		**Excellent**

___ 1.1 Children are not screened for the purpose of identifying special needs.*

___ 3.1 D All children, birth to 5 years of age, are screened for the purpose of identifying special needs.*

___ 5.1 D All children, birth to 5 years of age, are screened using a valid and reliable screening tool (e.g., Ages and Stages, Brigance, Early Screening Inventory).*

___ 7.1 D To protect against misidentification, safeguards are built into the screening process.**

___ 1.2 Parental consent is not obtained prior to screening (N/A is allowed when another organization conducts the screening and is responsible for obtaining parental consent).

___ 3.2 D Parental consent is obtained prior to screening (N/A is allowed when another organization conducts the screening and is responsible for obtaining parental consent).

___ 5.2 D Parents are informed of the results of screening.

___ 7.2 D Parents are involved in developing any special plans for their children based on the screening, and such plans are documented in the children's files.***

___ 5.3 D Children identified in the screening process as having possible special needs are referred to specialists for further evaluation (e.g., physician, physical therapist, or child study team).

___ 7.3 D A system is in place to support collaboration with specialists working with children with special needs.****

Rationale:

Circle the final score based on the scoring rules on pages 4–5.

1   2   3   4   5   6   7

10. Screening and Identification of Special Needs

11. Assessment in Support of Learning

Notes	Guiding Questions
* *Valid and reliable assessments* refers to research-based tools (e.g., High/Scope COR, Work Sampling System, or Teaching Strategies GOLD). ** *Standards* are published professional standards (e.g., NAEYC, NSACCA, or Head Start Child Development and Early Learning Framework) or individual state early learning standards. *Curriculum* refers to a framework that guides the intentional implementation of activities in support of children's learning and development. *** Aggregated assessment results are obtained when individual children's assessments are combined for the purpose of analysis (i.e., looking for trends to inform program improvement efforts).	How do teaching staff assess children's learning and development? • What assessment tools are used? Are they teacher-made? Are they valid and reliable? • What age groups of children are assessed? • Are there any additional ways teachers assess children's learning and development? How is the curriculum planned? • How are standards considered? • How are individual child assessment results used by teachers in lesson or activity planning? • How are aggregated assessment results used to evaluate or make long-range plans for the program?

11. Assessment in Support of Learning

1	2	3	4	5	6	7
Inadequate		**Minimal**		**Good**		**Excellent**

___ 1.1 Teaching staff do not use an assessment tool to assess children's learning and development.

___ 3.1 D Teaching staff use an assessment tool to assess children's learning and development.

___ 5.1 D Teaching staff use a valid and reliable assessment tool to assess children, birth to 5 years of age.*

___ 7.1 D Teaching staff use additional measures to assess children's learning and development (e.g., portfolios of children's work, teacher's observation notes).

___ 1.2 Standards are not considered in curriculum planning.**

___ 3.2 D Standards are considered in curriculum planning.**

___ 5.2 D Individual child assessment results are utilized by teaching staff in lesson or activity planning.

___ 7.2 D Aggregated child assessment results are utilized by administrative staff in long-range planning and/or program evaluation.***

Adapted from *Best Practices in Early Childhood Assessment* and used with permission of Judy Harris Helm, Best Practices, Inc.

Rationale:

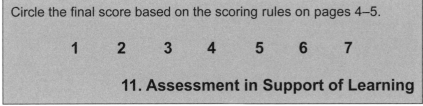

Circle the final score based on the scoring rules on pages 4–5.

1   2   3   4   5   6   7

11. Assessment in Support of Learning

Fiscal Management

12. Budget Planning

Notes	Guiding Questions

Notes

* Expenditures need to reflect the written goals; revenue needs to match or exceed expenditures.

** Use the following grid to determine when the fourth quarter begins:

Fiscal year begins	Fourth quarter begins
January 1	October 1
July 1	April 1
October 1	July 1

*** Quarterly cash-flow projections are developed from the operating budget and provide a summary of anticipated revenue and expenditures at three-month intervals.

Accepted practices that provide for adequate cash flow **may** include:
- ❏ the prompt deposit of income
- ❏ methods for informing parents about money owed
- ❏ clear written policies and procedures regarding the collection of delinquent tuition/fees
- ❏ clear written policies and procedures to maintain adequate attendance levels
- ❏ other _____

Guiding Questions

How is the program's operating budget prepared?
- Is the Administrator involved? How?
- Is a needs assessment conducted for the program?
- Are goals based on the needs assessment?
- Do the needs-assessment and goal-setting processes relate to the budgeting process? How?
- Does the budget reflect adequate resources to achieve program goals?

Does the Administrator have access to the program's current year operating budget? How detailed is the budget?
- Does it include both revenue and expenditures?
- Are there line-item breakdowns? How are these used?
- When is the projected operating budget for the next fiscal year available?

How effective is the budget in maintaining adequate cash flow?
- Are payroll, insurance, and taxes paid on time?
- Does the budget include a line item for deferred maintenance, equipment replacement, and/or capital improvements?
- How are cash-flow projections developed and used?
- What additional practices are in place to ensure adequate cash flow?

Fiscal Management

12. Budget Planning

1	2	3	4	5	6	7
Inadequate		**Minimal**		**Good**		**Excellent**

___ 1.1 The Administrator is not involved in developing the program's operating budget.

___ 3.1 The Administrator is involved in developing the program's operating budget.

___ 5.1 D Needs assessment and goal setting are an integral part of the program's budget-planning process.

___ 7.1 D The operating budget includes sufficient resources to achieve the program's written goals.*

___ 1.2 The current year operating budget, including revenue and expenditures, is not available.

___ 3.2 D The current year operating budget, including revenue and expenditures, is available.

___ 5.2 D The current year operating budget has line-item breakdowns to permit monitoring of revenue and expenditures.

___ 7.2 D A projected operating budget for the next fiscal year is available by the beginning of the fourth quarter of the current fiscal year.**

___ 1.3 Payroll, insurance, and taxes are not always paid on time.

___ 3.3 Payroll, insurance, and taxes are always paid on time.

___ 5.3 D The budget reflects deferred maintenance, equipment replacement, and/or capital improvements.

___ 7.3 D Quarterly cash-flow projections **and** at least two other accepted practices provide for adequate cash flow.***

Rationale:

Circle the final score based on the scoring rules on pages 4–5.

1   2   3   4   5   6   7

12. Budget Planning

13. Accounting Practices

Notes	Guiding Questions

*   Checks and balances **may** include:
     ❐ two or more signatures required on checks
     ❐ separation of restricted funds (e.g., grants, endowment, and major capital funds) from general operating funds
     ❐ a separation of duties (e.g., the same person does not receive cash and authorize cash disbursements)
     ❐ other _____
 	
**   *Independent* means that the reviewer is not an employee of the organization. A board member or parent can conduct an independent review.
	How are income and expense statements generated?
	   • How frequently are they generated?
	   • How is the Administrator involved?
	   • How does the Administrator use the income and expense statements?
	
	What are some examples of accounting checks-and-balances utilized by the organization?
	
	How are accounting records reviewed?
	   • Who is involved?
	   • How frequently do reviews occur?
	   • Is there an outside audit conducted? By whom?

34

13. Accounting Practices

1	2	3	4	5	6	7
Inadequate		**Minimal**		**Good**		**Excellent**

___ 1.1 An income and expense statement is not generated quarterly.

___ 3.1 D An income and expense statement is generated quarterly.

___ 5.1 D The Administrator has access to or generates quarterly income and expense statements.

___ 7.1 D The Administrator compares quarterly income and expense statements to quarterly cash-flow projections to monitor the center's fiscal status.

___ 1.2 There are no examples of accounting checks-and-balances.*

___ 3.2 D There is one example of accounting checks-and-balances.*

___ 5.2 D There are two examples of accounting checks-and-balances.*

___ 7.2 D There are three examples of accounting checks-and-balances.*

___ 1.3 There is no independent review of the accounting records (e.g., reconciliation of the bank statements, annual audit).**

___ 3.3 There is an independent review of the accounting records (e.g., reconciliation of the bank statements, annual audit).**

___ 5.3 D There is a quarterly review of the accounting records by an independent third party who has accounting or bookkeeping expertise.**

___ 7.3 D An outside audit is conducted annually by a certified public accountant.

Rationale:

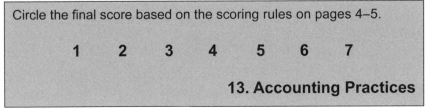

Circle the final score based on the scoring rules on pages 4–5.

1   2   3   4   5   6   7

13. Accounting Practices

Program Planning and Evaluation

14. Program Evaluation

Notes	Guiding Questions
* Examples of additional ways to obtain feedback from staff **may** include: ❏ suggestion box ❏ message book ❏ informal questionnaire ❏ organizational climate assessment ❏ notice of availability of Administrator to meet with staff ❏ agenda item at staff meetings ❏ exit interviews ❏ other _____ ** Examples of additional ways to obtain feedback from parents **may** include: ❏ suggestion box ❏ message book ❏ informal questionnaire ❏ notice of availability of Administrator to meet with parents ❏ agenda item at family meetings ❏ exit interviews ❏ other _____	How do staff evaluate the program? • Is an assessment tool used? • How frequently does program evaluation occur? • Are there any other ways for staff to provide feedback about program quality? How do parents evaluate the program? • Is an assessment tool used? • How frequently does program evaluation occur? • Are there any other ways for parents to provide feedback about program quality? How is the information obtained from staff and parent evaluations used? • How does this information influence program decision making? • Are written plans developed as a result of program evaluations from staff and parents? What are some examples? • How do staff and parents learn about how their feedback is used?

Program Planning and Evaluation

14. Program Evaluation

1	2	3	4	5	6	7
Inadequate		Minimal		Good		Excellent

___ 1.1 No assessment tool is used by staff to evaluate the program.

___ 3.1 D An assessment tool is used by staff to evaluate the program.

___ 5.1 D An assessment tool is used annually by staff to evaluate the program.

___ 7.1 D The center uses two or more ways to obtain feedback from staff in addition to using an assessment tool annually.*

___ 1.2 No assessment tool is used by parents to evaluate the program.

___ 3.2 D An assessment tool is used by parents to evaluate the program.

___ 5.2 D An assessment tool is used annually by parents to evaluate the program.

___ 7.2 D The center uses two or more ways to obtain feedback from parents in addition to using an assessment tool annually.**

___ 1.3 Program decision making is not influenced by staff and parent evaluations of the program.

___ 3.3 Program decision making is influenced by staff and parent evaluations of the program.

___ 5.3 D Data from staff and parent evaluations are used to develop a written plan for program improvement.

___ 7.3 D The center's evaluation process includes a feedback loop to staff and parents, reinforcing the value of their input.

Rationale:

Circle the final score based on the scoring rules on pages 4–5.

1   2   3   4   5   6   7

14. Program Evaluation

15. Strategic Planning

Notes	Guiding Questions
Evidence of strategic planning (a written mission or vision statement and a written business or strategic plan) must specifically address the early care and education program.	Does the center have a written mission or vision statement? • Does it specifically address early care and education? • Who was involved in developing or reviewing it? • How frequently is it reviewed?
* A *mission* is a succinct statement of the center's purpose for existence that informs strategic decision making.	Does the center have a written business or strategic plan? • Does it specifically address early care and education? • What does it include? • Who was involved in developing it? • How frequently is it reviewed and who is involved?
A *vision* is a statement of an ideal that can be used to motivate, inspire, and guide the center toward a desired future state.	

** The business or strategic plan is a document that **must** include:
      ❑ needs assessment
      ❑ plan for services
      ❑ short- and long-term goals
      ❑ strategies to achieve goals (e.g., marketing, enrollment, compensation, or financial plans)	

15. Strategic Planning

	1	2		3	4		5	6		7
	Inadequate			**Minimal**			**Good**			**Excellent**

___ 1.1 The center does not have a written mission or vision statement.*

___ 3.1 D The center has a written mission or vision statement.*

___ 5.1 D Staff and the center's governing/advisory board were involved in developing or reviewing the written mission or vision statement.*

___ 7.1 D The center's mission or vision statement is reviewed at least every five years by staff and the center's governing/advisory board.*

___ 1.2 The center does not have a written business plan or strategic plan.

___ 3.2 D The center has a written business plan or strategic plan.**

___ 5.2 D Staff and the center's governing/advisory board were involved in developing the written business plan or strategic plan.**

___ 7.2 D The center's written business plan or strategic plan is reviewed annually by staff and the center's governing/advisory board to evaluate progress in achieving goals.**

Rationale:

Circle the final score based on the scoring rules on pages 4–5.

1	2	3	4	5	6	7

15. Strategic Planning

Family Partnerships

16. Family Communications

Notes	Questions

Notes

* Orientation procedures **must** include providing families with written information regarding:
- ❑ center operations
- ❑ schedule
- ❑ fees
- ❑ calendar
- ❑ health requirements
- ❑ discipline policy

Orientation procedures **must** also include soliciting information from families about the child's:
- ❑ developmental history
- ❑ strengths
- ❑ likes
- ❑ dislikes

** Enhanced orientation procedures **must** include:
- ❑ a guided tour of the center
- ❑ an introduction to the teaching staff
- ❑ an opportunity to ask questions of the Administrator
- ❑ information about the center's family-friendly supports

*** A system to check in with new families **must** include:
- ❑ tangible, concrete evidence
- ❑ multiple individuals
- ❑ a defined process of accountability

**** Modes of communication **may** include:
- ❑ informal conversation
- ❑ family meetings
- ❑ newsletters
- ❑ bulletin board
- ❑ notes that go home with children
- ❑ mailed letters
- ❑ e-mail
- ❑ phone calls
- ❑ website
- ❑ other _____

***** A system to support daily communication between teaching staff and families **must** include:
- ❑ tangible, concrete evidence
- ❑ multiple individuals
- ❑ a defined process of accountability

Questions

How are new families oriented to the center?
- What written materials do they receive?
- What information is asked of families about their children?
- What practices are part of the orientation?
- Is there a system to check in with newly enrolled families?

How do staff create and maintain open communication with families about their beliefs, culture, and childrearing practices?
- When does this occur?
- How has the program made changes or implemented special plans for children to achieve consistency with their experiences at home?

How do staff communicate with families?
- What are the various ways the center communicates with families?
- Do any families speak a primary language other than the language spoken by staff? If so, how do staff communicate with those families?

Does the center provide opportunities for families to discuss their children's learning and development?
- Are there formal conferences? How often? How are the times for conferences scheduled?
- Is there a system to support daily communication between teaching staff and families?

Family Partnerships

16. Family Communications

1	2	3	4	5	6	7
Inadequate		**Minimal**		**Good**		**Excellent**

___ 1.1 The center does not have an orientation procedure for new families.

___ 3.1 D The center has an orientation procedure for new families.*

___ 5.1 D The center has enhanced family orientation procedures.**

___ 7.1 D The center has a system to check in with new families within 45 days of enrollment.***

___ 1.2 The staff do not ask families about their beliefs, culture, and childrearing practices.

___ 3.2 D The staff ask families about their beliefs, culture, and childrearing practices during the intake process.

___ 5.2 D The family's perspective about childrearing and cultural practices is solicited during parent meetings or conferences to support open communication.

___ 7.2 D The center implements procedures to achieve consistency between home and center when possible (e.g., adjusts child's nap, changes menu).

___ 1.3 The center does not communicate with families in their primary language or utilize resources as needed to communicate with families.

___ 3.3 The center communicates with families in their primary language or utilizes resources as needed to communicate with families.

___ 5.3 D The center regularly communicates with families by using six or more modes of communication.****

___ 7.3 D The center regularly communicates with families by using eight or more modes of communication.****

___ 1.4 The center does not provide formal conferencing to discuss children's learning and development.

___ 3.4 D The center provides one formal conference per year to discuss children's learning and development at times that are convenient for working families.

___ 5.4 D The center provides two formal conferences per year to discuss children's learning and development at times that are convenient for working families.

___ 7.4 D A system exists to support daily communication between teaching staff and families.*****

Rationale:

Circle the final score based on the scoring rules on pages 4–5.

1	2	3	4	5	6	7

16. Family Communications

17. Family Support and Involvement

Notes	Guiding Questions

* *Family support* refers to the variety of ways that a center can be responsive to family needs. Examples of family-friendly supports **may** include:
   ❏ children's book or toy lending library
   ❏ family resource library
   ❏ child care for sick or mildly ill children
   ❏ extended care during evenings or weekends
   ❏ information and/or referral to supportive services regarding family issues
   ❏ convenience services (e.g., take-home meals, photographs)
   ❏ adult classes (e.g., literacy, computer)
   ❏ home visits
   ❏ family meetings, seminars, or support groups
   ❏ social functions for families and staff
   ❏ child care during parent conferences or meetings
   ❏ provision for food or clothing donations
   ❏ transportation to and from the center
   ❏ tuition scholarships
   ❏ discount coupons for community events or services
   ❏ other _____
	What supports are offered to families?
	
	Are families invited to visit their children in the classroom?
	   • At what times?
	   • Are extended family members welcome?
	
	In what ways are family members involved in center activities?
	   • What are some events families attend?
	   • What are some routine classroom activities in which families participate?
	   • In what ways do families participate in decision making? Are they part of an advisory or governing board?

17. Family Support and Involvement

1	2	3	4	5	6	7
Inadequate		**Minimal**		**Good**		**Excellent**

___ 1.1 The center offers no family supports.*

___ 1.2 Parents are not invited to visit in the classroom.

___ 1.3 There is no plan for involving families in the activities of the center.

___ 3.1 D The center offers at least three family supports.*

___ 3.2 D Parents are invited to visit in the classroom.

___ 3.3 D Families participate in educational meetings, special events, parties, and/or fieldtrips.

___ 5.1 D The center offers at least five family supports.*

___ 5.2 D Parents are invited to visit in the classroom at any time.

___ 5.3 D Families participate in routine classroom activities (e.g., reading books, assisting with story dictation, helping with art projects).

___ 7.1 D The center offers at least seven family supports.*

___ 7.2 D Extended family members (e.g., grandparents, aunts, uncles) are welcome to visit in the classroom.

___ 7.3 D Family members serve on the center's governing/advisory board.

Rationale:

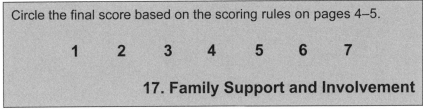

Circle the final score based on the scoring rules on pages 4–5.

1   2   3   4   5   6   7

17. Family Support and Involvement

18. External Communications

Notes	Guiding Questions
* Public relations tools **may** include: ❑ stationery ❑ brochure ❑ logo ❑ business cards ❑ signage ❑ newsletter ❑ website ❑ social networking page ❑ advertising copy ❑ phonebook advertisement ❑ promotional items (e.g., clothing, mugs, caps) ❑ other _____ ** *Projects a professional image* means that the center uses a consistent logo on all promotional materials and that the promotional materials are neat and grammatically correct. A proper noun (e.g., Kids' Korner) is an exception to this rule. *** *Multiple stakeholders* require that there be at least one representative from a minimum of two different stakeholder groups.	What are the various public relations tools utilized by the center? Do the public relations tools project a professional image? • Is the logo and contact information consistent? • Is information grammatically correct? • Are they reviewed to assure information is current? • How often are they reviewed? Who is involved? What happens when a prospective family calls to inquire about the program? • How quickly is follow-up information sent or communicated? • Are records kept of inquiries? How are these records used? • Are staff trained to respond to inquiries? Is there a written guide?

Marketing and Public Relations

18. External Communications

	1	2	3	4	5	6	7
	Inadequate		**Minimal**		**Good**		**Excellent**

___ 1.1 The center utilizes fewer than three public relations tools.*

___ 1.2 Public relations tools do not project a professional image.**

___ 1.3 Information about the center is not sent out, nor are follow-up calls made in response to inquiries within one business day.

___ 3.1 D The center utilizes three or more public relations tools.*

___ 3.2 D Public relations tools project a professional image.**

___ 3.3 Information about the center is sent out and/or follow-up calls are made in response to inquiries within one business day.

___ 5.1 D The center utilizes five or more public relations tools.*

___ 5.2 D Public relations tools are reviewed to ensure that content is not outdated.

___ 5.3 D Records are kept of all prospective families who inquire about the center and the follow-up action taken (e.g., call made, letter sent).

___ 7.1 D The center utilizes seven or more public relations tools.*

___ 7.2 D There was a review by multiple stakeholders (e.g., parents, staff, board) of the public relations tools within the last three years.***

___ 7.3 D The center has a written guide to train staff in providing information to prospective families who call or visit.

Rationale:

Circle the final score based on the scoring rules on pages 4–5.

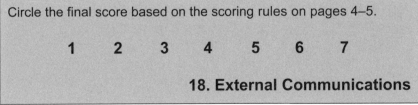

1   2   3   4   5   6   7

18. External Communications

19. Community Outreach

Notes	Guiding Questions
* *Local community organization* refers to a business, civic, or faith-based organization that is not primarily concerned with early care and education. Examples of local community organizations **may** include: ❐ Rotary International ❐ chamber of commerce ❐ League of Women Voters ❐ business roundtable ❐ United Way ❐ community development agency ❐ YWCA, YMCA ❐ church, synagogue, mosque, or temple ❐ other _____ ** *Leadership role* means that the Administrator and/or center staff chair a committee, serve on an advisory/governing board, or hold office. *** *Involvement* means that the Administrator and/or center staff participate in a directors' network, are members of a national or local early childhood organization, or collaborate with the local elementary school to ensure smooth transitions. **** *Active role* means the Administrator and/or center staff attend meetings regularly.	In what ways are the Administrator and/or center staff involved with local community organizations? • Do they attend events sponsored by local community organizations? • Are they members of local community organizations? • Do they play a leadership role? What do the Administrator and/or the center staff do to promote positive relations with the immediate neighborhood or local community? • What are some strategies used to promote positive relations? • How is the center supported by the immediate neighborhood or local community? In what ways are the Administrator and/or center staff involved in the early childhood professional community? • Are they members of an early childhood organization? • Do they attend meetings regularly? • Have they chaired a committee or held office? If so, when?

19. Community Outreach

1	2	3	4	5	6	7
Inadequate		**Minimal**		**Good**		**Excellent**

___ 1.1 The Administrator or center staff do not attend two or more events per year sponsored by a local community organization.*

___ 3.1 The Administrator and/or center staff attend two or more events per year sponsored by a local community organization.*

___ 5.1 D The Administrator and/or center staff are members of a local community organization.*

___ 7.1 D The Administrator and/or center staff play a leadership role in a local community organization.**

___ 1.2 The Administrator or center staff appear indifferent to the center's impact on the immediate neighborhood or local community.

___ 3.2 The Administrator and/or center staff show concern about being good neighbors (e.g., post reminders to families and visitors about parking restrictions, maintain clean sidewalks).

___ 5.2 D The Administrator and/or center staff seek opportunities to build good relations within the immediate neighborhood or local community (e.g., inviting neighbors to open houses, using neighborhood resources for special projects).

___ 7.2 D There is evidence of support from the immediate neighborhood or local community (e.g., financial support, in-kind donated services, tangible gifts, discounted services, letters of support).

___ 1.3 The Administrator or center staff have no involvement in the early childhood professional community.***

___ 3.3 D The Administrator and/or center staff have some involvement in the early childhood professional community.***

___ 5.3 D The Administrator and/or center staff play an active role in the early childhood professional community.****

___ 7.3 D The Administrator and/or center staff played a leadership role in the early childhood professional community during the past three years.**

Rationale:

Circle the final score based on the scoring rules on pages 4–5.

1   2   3   4   5   6   7

19. Community Outreach

Technology

20. Technological Resources

Notes	Guiding Questions
* *Functional computer* refers to a computer that effectively runs programs for word processing, spreadsheet, database, and presentation graphics.	Do staff have access to computers and printers at work? • How many computers are available? • Who has access to them? • When do teaching staff have access? Does the center have Internet access? • Who has access to the Internet? • When do teaching staff have access to the Internet?

Technology

20. Technological Resources

1	2	3	4	5	6	7
Inadequate		**Minimal**		**Good**		**Excellent**

___ 1.1 The center does not have a functional computer and printer.*

___ 3.1 The center has a functional
O computer and printer.*

___ 5.1 The center has multiple
O functional computers that are available to teaching staff as well as administrative staff.*

___ 7.1 Teaching staff have access to
O functional computers during their planning and preparation time.*

___ 1.2 The center does not have Internet access.

___ 3.2 The center has Internet access.
O

___ 5.2 The center has Internet access
O for teaching staff as well as administrative staff.

___ 7.2 The center has Internet access
O available to teaching staff during their planning and preparation time.

Rationale:

Circle the final score based on the scoring rules on pages 4–5.

1   2   3   4   5   6   7

20. Technological Resources

21. Use of Technology

Notes	Guiding Questions
* Examples of use of technology for recordkeeping **may** include: ❑ enrollment ❑ accounts receivable, accounts payable ❑ budget ❑ cash-flow projections ❑ employee benefits ❑ inventory monitoring ❑ database ❑ other _____ ** Examples of use of technology for communication **may** include: ❑ letter ❑ presentation ❑ memo ❑ newsletter ❑ e-mail ❑ marketing material ❑ website ❑ other _____ *** Examples of technology used by teaching staff **may** include: ❑ voice recorder ❑ computer ❑ camera ❑ television ❑ camcorder ❑ DVD player ❑ scanner ❑ other _____ ❑ music player **** A *comprehensive technology policy* **must** include specific written guidelines for staff regarding: ❑ use of social media (e.g., Facebook, Twitter) ❑ e-mail etiquette ❑ personal use of the center's technology resources ❑ digital confidentiality of work-related information ❑ use of media releases (e.g., permission to use image, voice, and/or name in various media projects)	How do administrative staff use technology in their work? • What are some examples of use for recordkeeping? • What are some examples of use for communication? • What types of technology training have staff participated in? • When was the last time administrative staff participated in technology training? How do teaching staff use technology in their work? • What are some ways technology is used when working with children and families? • How frequently do teaching staff use technology in their work with children and families? • When was the last time teaching staff participated in technology training? Does the center have a written policy regarding staff use of technology? • What does it include?

21. Use of Technology

1	2	3	4	5	6	7
Inadequate		**Minimal**		**Good**		**Excellent**

___ 1.1 Administrative staff do not use technology in their work.

___ 3.1 D Administrative staff use technology for recordkeeping (provide at least three examples).*

___ 5.1 D Administrative staff use technology for communication (provide at least three examples).**

___ 7.1 D Job-specific technology training was provided for administrative staff within the past year.

___ 1.2 Teaching staff do not use technology in their work with children and families.

___ 3.2 D Teaching staff use technology in their work with children and families (provide at least three examples).***

___ 5.2 D Teaching staff use technology in their work with children and families at least once a week (e.g., documentation of children's learning, child assessment, calendar).***

___ 7.2 D Job-specific technology training was provided for teaching staff within the past year.

___ 1.3 There is no written policy regarding the staff use of technology.

___ 3.3 D There is a written policy regarding the staff use of technology.

___ 5.3 D The written technology policy includes the acceptable or unacceptable use of computer, e-mail, and cell phone or other mobile device.

___ 7.3 D There is a written comprehensive technology policy.****

Rationale:

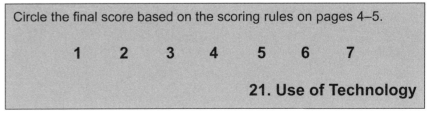

Circle the final score based on the scoring rules on pages 4–5.

1   2   3   4   5   6   7

21. Use of Technology

Staff Qualifications

22. Administrator

Notes	Data Collection Procedures

Administrator refers to the individual who has primary responsibility for planning, implementing, and evaluating the early childhood program. The Administrator must be located on-site if the center has four or more classrooms or a total enrollment of 60 or more full-time equivalent (FTE) children. Role titles for the Administrator vary and may include director, manager, coordinator, or principal.

Depending on the type and size of the early childhood program, there may be several individuals who have administrative roles. The rating for this item is based only on the background and qualifications of the individual designated as the Administrator. The *Program Administration Scale* does not include assessment of other administrative roles such as assistant director or education coordinator.

* *Management experience* refers to the responsibility for early childhood or school-age program planning, implementation, and evaluation. It can include experience as an assistant director or coordinator of a program component. A *year of experience* is defined as a minimum of 1,200 hours (a six-hour workday for an academic year).

** *Professional contributions* refer to activities that show the Administrator's commitment to the field of early childhood beyond center-based responsibilities. These may include service or leadership in an early childhood professional organization, serving as a resource to the media about early childhood issues, presenting at professional conferences, providing training for another program, mentoring an individual from another program, advocacy, research, and writing/publishing.

Use the **Administrator Qualifications Worksheet** on page 62 to record information regarding the Administrator's general education, specialized training, experience, and professional contributions. This data can then be used to rate the indicators on the following page and generate an item score for Item 22.

Staff Qualifications

22. Administrator

	1		2		3		4		5		6		7
	Inadequate				**Minimal**				**Good**				**Excellent**

___ 1.1 The Administrator has less than an associate's degree **or** 60 sh of college credit.

___ 1.2 The Administrator has less than 18 sh of college credit for ECE/CD coursework.

___ 1.3 The Administrator has no college credit for management coursework.

___ 1.4 The Administrator has less than one year of management experience.*

___ 3.1 D The Administrator has an associate's degree **or** 60 sh of college credit.

___ 3.2 D The Administrator has 21 or more sh of college credit for ECE/CD coursework.

___ 3.3 D The Administrator has 9 or more sh of college credit for management coursework.

___ 3.4 D The Administrator has one or more years of management experience.*

___ 5.1 D The Administrator has a bachelor's degree.

___ 5.2 D The Administrator has 24 or more sh of college credit for ECE/CD coursework.

___ 5.3 D The Administrator has 15 or more sh of college credit for management coursework.

___ 5.4 D The Administrator has three or more years of management experience.*

___ 5.5 D The Administrator has made four or more professional contributions during the past three years.**

___ 7.1 D The Administrator has a master's **or** other advanced degree.

___ 7.2 D The Administrator has 30 or more sh of college credit for ECE/CD coursework.

___ 7.3 D The Administrator has 21 or more sh of college credit for management coursework.

___ 7.4 D The Administrator has five or more years of management experience.*

___ 7.5 D The Administrator has made six or more professional contributions during the past three years.**

Rationale:

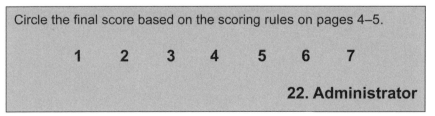

Circle the final score based on the scoring rules on pages 4–5.

1   2   3   4   5   6   7

22. Administrator

23. Lead Teacher

Notes	Data Collection Procedures
Depending on the staffing pattern of the program, there may be several individuals working with a group of children who are responsible for their daily care and education.	1. Make copies of the **Teaching Staff Qualifications Worksheet** on page 63 so there is a separate worksheet for each group/classroom of children. At the top of the worksheet write the name of the group/classroom.
Lead Teacher refers to the individual with the highest professional qualifications assigned to teach a group of children and who is responsible for daily lesson planning, parent conferences, child assessment, and curriculum planning. This individual may also supervise other members of the teaching team. In some settings, this person is called a head teacher, master teacher, or teacher.	2. In the designated space, write the initials of each member of the teaching staff regularly assigned to each group/classroom. This worksheet provides space for up to four members of the teaching staff for each group/classroom.
* A *year of experience* is defined as a minimum of 1,200 hours (a six-hour workday for an academic year).	3. Provide the information regarding the education, specialized training, and experience of each member of the teaching staff regularly assigned to each group/classroom.
	4. Determine which member of the teaching staff for each group/classroom will be designated as the Lead Teacher for purposes of completing Item 23.
	5. Make additional copies of Item 23 on page 55 so that each individual designated as Lead Teacher (one for each group/classroom of children) has a separate Item 23 page. Complete the rating of Item 23 for each Lead Teacher and transfer this score to Column A on the **Summary of Teaching Staff Qualifications Worksheet** on page 64.
	6. Determine the average score for Item 23 by summing the individual Lead Teacher scores and dividing by the number of Lead Teachers (the same as the number of groups/classrooms). Record this Item 23 Average Score on the bottom of the **Summary of Teaching Staff Qualifications Worksheet**.

23. Lead Teacher

1	2	3	4	5	6	7
Inadequate		**Minimal**		**Good**		**Excellent**

___ 1.1 Lead Teacher does not have an associate's degree **or** 60 sh of college credit.

___ 3.1 D Lead Teacher has an associate's degree **or** has 60 sh of college credit and is enrolled in a bachelor's degree program.

___ 5.1 D Lead Teacher has a bachelor's degree.

___ 7.1 D Lead Teacher has a master's **or** other advanced degree.

___ 1.2 Lead Teacher has less than 12 sh of college credit for ECE/CD coursework.

___ 3.2 D Lead Teacher has 21 or more sh of college credit for ECE/CD coursework.

___ 5.2 D Lead Teacher has 30 or more sh of college credit for ECE/CD coursework.

___ 7.2 D Lead Teacher has certification and is qualified to teach young children in a public school system.

___ 1.3 Lead Teacher has less than six months experience teaching young children (birth to 8 years of age).*

___ 3.3 D Lead Teacher has six or more months of experience teaching young children (birth to 8 years of age).*

___ 5.3 D Lead Teacher has one or more years of experience teaching young children (birth to 8 years of age).*

___ 7.3 D Lead Teacher has three or more years of experience teaching young children (birth to 8 years of age).*

Rationale:

Circle the final score based on the scoring rules on pages 4–5.

1   2   3   4   5   6   7

23. Lead Teacher

24. Teacher (N/A is allowed)

Notes	Data Collection Procedures

Teacher refers to a member of the teaching team who shares responsibility with the *Lead Teacher* for the care and education of an assigned group of children.

Depending on the staffing pattern of the program, there may be more than one person designated as Teacher for each group of children. It is also possible that a group of children will not have someone designated as Teacher on the teaching team.

* To rate 1.2 use the following formula:
    ❑ It is true, Teacher does not have a CDA.
    ❑ It is true, Teacher has less than 6 sh of college credit for ECE/CD coursework.

    If both are true, rating is *yes*
    If only one is true, rating is *no*
    If neither is true, rating is *no*

** A *year of experience* is defined as a minimum of 1,200 hours (a six-hour workday for an academic year).

The information needed to score this item is obtained from data recorded on the **Teaching Staff Qualifications Worksheet** on page 63 for each group/classroom of children.

1. Determine the total number of Teachers for the entire program and duplicate sufficient copies of Item 24 on page 57 so that each individual designated as a Teacher has a separate Item 24 page.

2. Using the information recorded on the **Teaching Staff Qualifications Worksheet**, rate the indicators for Item 24 for each Teacher.

3. Transfer the individual Teacher Item 24 scores to Column B on the **Summary of Teaching Staff Qualifications Worksheet** on page 64.

4. Determine the average score for Item 24 by summing the individual Teacher scores and dividing by the number of Teachers. Record this Item 24 Average Score on the bottom of the **Summary of Teaching Staff Qualifications Worksheet**.

24. Teacher (N/A is allowed)

1	2	3	4	5	6	7
Inadequate		**Minimal**		**Good**		**Excellent**

___ 1.1 Teacher has less than 30 sh of college credit.

___ 3.1 D Teacher has 30 or more sh of college credit.

___ 5.1 D Teacher has an associate's degree **or** 60 or more sh of college credit.

___ 7.1 D Teacher has 60 or more sh of college credit **and** is enrolled in a bachelor's degree program.

___ 1.2 Teacher does not have a CDA credential **and** has less than 6 sh of college credit for ECE/CD coursework.*

___ 3.2 D Teacher has a CDA credential **or** 12 or more sh of college credit for ECE/CD coursework.

___ 5.2 D Teacher has 21 or more sh of college credit for ECE/CD coursework.

___ 7.2 D Teacher has 30 or more sh of college credit for ECE/CD coursework.

___ 5.3 D Teacher has one or more years of experience working with young children (birth to 8 years of age) in a group setting.**

___ 7.3 D Teacher has two or more years of experience working with young children (birth to 8 years of age) in a group setting.**

Rationale:

Circle the final score based on the scoring rules on pages 4–5.

1	2	3	4	5	6	7	N/A

24. Teacher

25. Assistant Teacher/Aide (N/A is allowed)

Notes	Data Collection Procedures

Assistant Teacher/Aide refers to a member of the teaching team assigned to a group of children who works under the direct supervision of the Lead Teacher and/or Teacher.
 	
Depending on the staffing pattern of the program, there may be more than one person designated as Assistant Teacher/Aide for each group or classroom of children. It is also possible that a group or classroom of children will not have any assigned Assistant Teachers/Aides.
 	
* To rate 1.2 use the following formula:
   ❐ It is true, Assistant Teacher/Aide has no college credit for ECE/CD coursework.
   ❐ It is true, Assistant Teacher/Aide is not enrolled in ECE/CD college coursework.
 	
   If both are true, rating is *yes*
   If only one is true, rating is *no*
   If neither is true, rating is *no*
 	
** A *year of experience* is defined as a minimum of 1,200 hours (a six-hour workday for an academic year).
	The information needed to score this item is obtained from data recorded on the **Teaching Staff Qualifications Worksheet** on page 63 for each group/classroom of children.
	
	1. Determine the total number of Assistant Teachers/Aides for the entire program and duplicate sufficient copies of Item 25 on page 59 so that each individual designated as an Assistant Teacher/Aide has a separate Item 25 page.
	
	2. Using the information recorded on the **Teaching Staff Qualifications Worksheet**, rate the indicators for Item 25 for each Assistant Teacher/Aide.
	
	3. Transfer the individual Assistant Teacher/Aide Item 25 scores to Column C on the **Summary of Teaching Staff Qualifications Worksheet** on page 64.
	
	4. Determine the average score for Item 25 by summing the individual Assistant Teacher/Aide scores and dividing by the number of Assistant Teachers/Aides. Record this Item 25 Average Score on the bottom of the **Summary of Teaching Staff Qualifications Worksheet**.

25. Assistant Teacher/Aide (N/A is allowed)

1	2	3	4	5	6	7
Inadequate		**Minimal**		**Good**		**Excellent**

___ 1.1 Assistant Teacher/Aide does not have a high school diploma or GED.

___ 1.2 Assistant Teacher/Aide has no college credit for ECE/CD coursework **and** is not enrolled in ECE/CD college coursework.*

___ 3.1 Assistant Teacher/Aide has a high school diploma or GED.

___ 3.2 Assistant Teacher/Aide has
D 3 or more sh of college credit for ECE/CD coursework **or** is enrolled in ECE/CD college coursework.

___ 5.1 Assistant Teacher/Aide has
D 9 or more sh of college credit.

___ 5.2 Assistant Teacher/Aide has
D 6 or more sh of college credit for ECE/CD coursework.

___ 5.3 Assistant Teacher/Aide has one
D or more years of supervised experience working with young children (birth to 8 years age) in a group setting.**

___ 7.1 Assistant Teacher/Aide has
D 15 or more sh of college credit.

___ 7.2 Assistant Teacher/Aide has
D 9 or more sh of college credit for ECE/CD coursework.

___ 7.3 Assistant Teacher/Aide
D has two or more years of supervised experience working with young children (birth to 8 years of age) in a group setting.**

Rationale:

Circle the final score based on the scoring rules on pages 4–5.

1   2   3   4   5   6   7   N/A

25. Assistant Teacher/Aide

Program Administration Scale
Worksheets and Forms

- **Administrator Qualifications Worksheet**

- **Teaching Staff Qualifications Worksheet**

- **Summary of Teaching Staff Qualifications Worksheet**

- **Item Summary**

- **PAS Profile**

Administrator Qualifications Worksheet

The Administrator is the individual who has primary responsibility for planning, implementing, and evaluating the early childhood program. The Administrator must be located on-site if the center has four or more classrooms or a total enrollment of 60 or more full-time equivalent (FTE) children. Role titles for the Administrator vary and may include director, manager, coordinator, or principal.

Program: _____ Administrator's name: _____

Highest Education Level

High School/GED ☐
Associate's degree ☐
Bachelor's degree ☐
Master's degree ☐
Doctorate ☐

General Education

_____ Total semester hours (sh) of college coursework

Specialized ECE/CD Coursework

_____ Total semester hours of ECE/CD coursework

Specialized Management Coursework*

_____ Total semester hours of management coursework

Administrator Credential

Holds administrator credential: ☐ Yes ☐ No
Type/level of credential: _____
Issued by: _____

Management Experience

years _____

months _____

Professional Contributions**   List professional contributions within the last three years:

1. _____   4. _____
2. _____   5. _____
3. _____   6. _____

---

* Examples of management coursework include: accounting, marketing, finance, communications, technology, leadership, staff development, and organizational change.

** Professional contributions refer to activities that show the Administrator's commitment to the field of early childhood beyond center-based responsibilities. These may include service or leadership in an early childhood professional organization, serving as a resource to the media about early childhood issues, presenting at professional conferences, providing training for another program, mentoring an individual from another program, advocacy, research, and writing/publishing.

Teaching Staff Qualifications Worksheet
(Lead Teachers, Teachers, Assistant Teachers/Aides)

Please complete one worksheet for each group/classroom (see instructions on pages 54, 56, and 58).

Program: _____   Group/classroom: _____

Teaching staff initials: _____   _____   _____   _____

Teaching role*: _____   _____   _____   _____

* Teaching Roles:

Lead Teacher (LT)
The individual with the highest professional qualifications assigned to teach a group of children and who is responsible for daily lesson planning, parent conferences, child assessment, and curriculum planning.

Teacher (T)
A member of the teaching team who shares responsibility with the Lead Teacher for the care and education of an assigned group of children.

Assistant Teacher/Aide (AT)
A member of the teaching team assigned to a group of children who works under the direct supervision of the Lead Teacher and/or Teacher.

Highest Education Level

High School/GED	☐	☐	☐	☐
Associate's degree	☐	☐	☐	☐
Bachelor's degree	☐	☐	☐	☐
Master's degree	☐	☐	☐	☐
Doctorate	☐	☐	☐	☐

General Education

Total semester hours (sh) of completed college coursework	___	___	___	___
Currently enrolled in a bachelor's degree program	☐	☐	☐	☐

Specialized Coursework

Total semester hours of completed ECE/CD coursework	___	___	___	___
Currently enrolled in ECE/CD college coursework	☐	☐	☐	☐

Credentials

CDA	☐	☐	☐	☐
State Teacher Certification	☐	☐	☐	☐

Teaching Experience

years	___	___	___	___
months	___	___	___	___

Summary of Teaching Staff Qualifications Worksheet

Program: _____   Date: _____

Group/Classroom Name	A Lead Teacher Item 23 Score	B Teacher Item 24 Score	C Assistant Teacher Item 25 Score
1. _____	_____	_____ _____ _____	_____ _____ _____
2. _____	_____	_____ _____ _____	_____ _____ _____
3. _____	_____	_____ _____ _____	_____ _____ _____
4. _____	_____	_____ _____ _____	_____ _____ _____
5. _____	_____	_____ _____ _____	_____ _____ _____

Sum of scores in Column A		**Sum of scores in Column B**		**Sum of scores in Column C**	
÷		÷		÷	
Number of scores in Column A		**Number of scores in Column B**		**Number of scores in Column C**	
=		=		=	
Item 23 Average Score		**Item 24 Average Score**		**Item 25 Average Score**	

64

Item Summary

Program: _____   Date: _____

Instructions

Use this form to summarize the item scores and to calculate the Total PAS Score and Average PAS Item Score.

- Enter the item scores in the spaces provided.

- Sum all the item scores and enter the total in the space provided. This is the Total PAS Score.

- Divide the Total PAS Score by the total number of items (minimum of 23 for all programs; 24 or 25 for programs that have a staffing pattern that includes Teachers and/or Assistant Teachers/Aides). The resulting number is the Average PAS Item Score.

Item	Score
1. Staff Orientation	_____
2. Supervision and Performance Appraisal	_____
3. Staff Development	_____
4. Compensation	_____
5. Benefits	_____
6. Staffing Patterns and Scheduling	_____
7. Facilities Management	_____
8. Risk Management	_____
9. Internal Communications	_____
10. Screening and Identification of Special Needs	_____
11. Assessment in Support of Learning	_____
12. Budget Planning	_____
13. Accounting Practices	_____
14. Program Evaluation	_____
15. Strategic Planning	_____
16. Family Communications	_____
17. Family Support and Involvement	_____
18. External Communications	_____
19. Community Outreach	_____
20. Technological Resources	_____
21. Use of Technology	_____
22. Administrator	_____
23. Lead Teacher	_____
24. Teacher (N/A is allowed)	_____
25. Assistant Teacher/Aide (N/A is allowed)	_____

Sum of item scores   [   ] ÷ [   ] = [   ]

| Total PAS Score | Number of items scored | Average PAS Item Score |

The Program Administration Scale Profile

Program: _____ Date: _____

Subscales	Items	1	2	3	4	5	6	7
Human Resources Development	1. Staff Orientation							
	2. Supervision and Performance Appraisal							
	3. Staff Development							
Personnel Cost and Allocation	4. Compensation							
	5. Benefits							
	6. Staffing Patterns and Scheduling							
Center Operations	7. Facilities Management							
	8. Risk Management							
	9. Internal Communications							
Child Assessment	10. Screening and Identification of Special Needs							
	11. Assessment in Support of Learning							
Fiscal Management	12. Budget Planning							
	13. Accounting Practices							
Program Planning and Evaluation	14. Program Evaluation							
	15. Strategic Planning							
Family Partnerships	16. Family Communications							
	17. Family Support and Involvement							
Marketing and Public Relations	18. External Communications							
	19. Community Outreach							
Technology	20. Technological Resources							
	21. Use of Technology							
Staff Qualifications	22. Administrator							
	23. Lead Teacher							
	24. Teacher (N/A is allowed)							
	25. Assistant Teacher/Aide (N/A is allowed)							

Total PAS Score _____ ÷ Number of items _____ = Average PAS Item Score _____

66

Program Administration Scale
Appendices

- **Psychometric Characteristics of the PAS**

- **References and Resources**

- **About the Authors**

Psychometric Characteristics of the PAS

Psychometric Criteria

The development of the *Program Administration Scale* was guided by seven psychometric criteria:

1. The PAS should measure distinct but related administrative practices of an early childhood program.

2. The PAS should be able to differentiate low- and high-quality programs.

3. The PAS should be applicable for use in different types of programs (e.g., for-profit, nonprofit, part-day, full-day, faith-based, military, Head Start, school-based, corporate-sponsored).

4. The PAS should be applicable for use in programs of varying sizes.

5. The PAS should demonstrate good internal consistency among scale items.

6. The PAS should demonstrate good inter-rater reliability.

7. The PAS should be easy to score and generate an easy-to-understand profile to support program improvement efforts.

Normative Samples

Two reliability and validity studies of the *Program Administration Scale* have been conducted by the authors. Sample #1 includes data collected in 2003 from 67 center-based early care and education programs in Illinois. Sample #2 includes data collected between 2006 and 2009 from 564 centers in 25 states.

Sample #1. The Illinois Network of Child Care Resource and Referral Agencies (INCCRRA) generated a list of all child care centers in Cook (Chicago), Cook (Suburban), Jackson, Madison, McLean, and Winnebago counties, including contact information and descriptive data on center capacity, NAEYC accreditation status, and legal auspices. The counties targeted for this sample were selected because they included urban, suburban, and rural geographic regions of the state.

The Metropolitan Chicago Information Center (MCIC) took the INCCRRA information and constructed a sample frame based on the center's NAEYC accreditation status (not accredited and accredited) and center size (small, medium, large). From a pool of 176 programs that provided adequate representation of each of the state's geographic areas, 124 centers were randomly contacted and asked to participate in a reliability and validity study of the PAS. A total of 67 centers agreed to participate and interviews with each on-site administrator were scheduled.

The mean licensed capacity of centers included in Sample #1 was 102 children. Centers employed, on average, 17 staff who worked more than ten hours per week. Thirty-two of the centers (48%) were accredited by the National Association for the Education of Young Children (NAEYC). Approximately two-thirds of the programs (67%) were nonprofit; one-third represented the for-profit sector. Twenty-two of the nonprofit programs received Head Start funding and five programs were sponsored by faith-based organizations.

Sample #2. The PAS assessments for Sample #2 were conducted as part of the McCormick Center for Early Childhood Leadership's national PAS assessor certification process. Assessors were trained over a four-day period and achieved an inter-rater reliability of 86% or higher with the PAS national anchors. Data for the 564 PAS assessments were collected within four months of completing reliability training. Only PAS data from assessments that met certification review criteria were included.

While data regarding the PAS items were collected on all programs, descriptive background information on some of the centers was not gathered. There is missing data in Sample #2 relating to program size and accreditation status for 12 programs. Information relating to funding sources and program type (legal auspices) were not collected for 68 programs.

The mean licensed capacity of centers included in Sample #2 was 90 children, with the average center caring for 64 children at least 35 hours a week. Centers employed, on average, 14 staff who worked more than ten hours per week. Approximately two-thirds of the programs (69%) were nonprofit; the remaining programs represented the for-profit sector. Thirty-five percent of programs in Sample #2 received Head Start funding, 36% received state prekindergarten funding, and 23% were affiliated with faith-based organizations.

Table 1 provides a distribution of the centers in Sample #2 by size and NAEYC accreditation status. Table 2 provides a distribution of the sample by program type (legal auspices).

Table 1. Distribution of Centers by Size and NAEYC Accreditation Status – Sample #2

Accreditation Status	Center Size						Total	
	small		medium		large			
	n	%	n	%	n	%	n	%
Not Accredited	138	25.0	105	19.0	137	25.0	380	69
Accredited	58	10.5	56	10.0	58	10.5	172	31
Total	196	35.5	161	29.0	195	35.5	552	100

Note: small = less than 60 children; medium = 60–100 children; large = more than 100 children

Table 2. Distribution of Centers by Program Type – Sample #2

Program Type	n	%
Nonprofit – part of agency or organization	205	41
Nonprofit – independent	144	29
For-profit – private proprietary or partnership	106	22
For-profit – corporation or chain (e.g., Kindercare, La Petite Academy)	31	6
For-profit – corporate sponsored (e.g., Bright Horizons Family Solutions)	10	2
Total	496	100

Reliability and Validity

Content validity. Content validity for the *Program Administration Scale* was initially established in 2003 by a panel of ten early childhood experts who evaluated each indicator, item, and subscale on the PAS to ensure that key leadership and management practices of center-based early childhood programs were included. Content reviewers were asked to respond to the following questions and provide feedback:

- Do the items under each subscale adequately describe the subscale?
- Do the indicators under each item adequately represent each item?
- Do the indicators appropriately show increasing levels of quality on a continuum?
- Does the wording of the item and subscale headings adequately reflect their content?

In addition to the content evaluation by ten early childhood experts, the *Program Administration Scale* was also reviewed informally by ten other early childhood administrators, consultants, and trainers. Multiple refinements were made to the wording and layout of the PAS as a result of the helpful feedback received from reviewers. Redundant indicators were deleted and the data-collection protocol was streamlined.

Since the publication of the first edition of the PAS in 2004, additional refinements have been made to the notes accompanying the PAS indicators based on feedback received from assessors who have visited programs and interviewed directors as part of PAS assessments in different regions of the country. This has helped ensure that the indicators continue to reflect best leadership and management practices in early care and education.

Descriptive statistics. Table 3 provides the mean scores and standard deviations for the 25 items rated using the 7-point scale of the PAS. There are a total of 81 indicator strands used to compute scores for the 25 items.

The Total PAS Score represented in Table 3 is the sum of the item mean scores. Because the 10 subscales of the PAS are used only as convenient headings for clustering items, and not as separate indicators of organizational effectiveness, mean scores for the subscales are not included on the profile that users generate to guide their program improvement efforts.

The Average PAS Item Score for Sample #2 is 3.47, with 33% of items scoring at level 1 (inadequate) and 15% scoring at level 7 (excellent). This suggests that the PAS has an acceptable distribution of item scores across the quality continuum. For Sample #1, the average Total PAS Score was 89.68 for the 25 items. The Average PAS Item Score was 3.59 with 29% of items rated at a level 1 and 13% rated at a level 7.

Table 3. Mean Scores and Standard Deviations for PAS Items – Sample #2 (N =564)

Item #	Item	Indicator Strands	M	SD
Human Resources Development				
1	Staff orientation	3	2.88	1.97
2	Supervision/performance appraisal	3	3.37	2.10
3	Staff development	3	4.01	2.12
Personnel Cost and Allocation				
4	Compensation	3	3.04	2.22
5	Benefits	5	2.00	1.61
6	Staffing patterns and scheduling	4	2.85	1.97
Center Operations				
7	Facilities management	3	4.99	1.93
8	Risk management	4	2.50	1.70
9	Internal communications	5	2.40	1.83
Child Assessment				
10	Screening/identification of special needs	3	4.50	2.55
11	Assessment in support of learning	2	5.50	2.21
Fiscal Management				
12	Budget planning	3	3.35	4.41
13	Accounting practices	3	3.61	2.45
Program Planning and Evaluation				
14	Program evaluation	3	3.62	2.30
15	Strategic planning	2	2.81	2.33
Family Partnerships				
16	Family communications	4	3.26	2.24
17	Family support and involvement	3	4.84	1.98
Marketing and Public Relations				
18	External communications	3	3.97	1.64
19	Community outreach	3	3.58	2.05
Technology				
20	Technological resources	2	3.68	2.35
21	Use of technology	3	4.90	2.18
Staff Qualifications				
22	Administrator	5	2.22	1.63
23	Lead Teacher*	3	2.65	1.42
24	Teacher**	3	2.78	1.82
25	Assistant Teacher/Aide***	3	3.50	2.20
Total PAS		**81**	**86.81**	**24.00**

*n = 2,589 lead teachers; ** n = 1,724 teachers; *** n =1,027 assistant teachers/aides

The slightly higher Total PAS Score and Average PAS Item Score for Sample #1 may be attributed to the higher items scores for Staff Qualifications for the Illinois sample. Requisite qualifications in Illinois are somewhat higher than elsewhere in the country. The difference is reflected in centers' higher ratings in the items comprising the Staff Qualifications subscale. The 67 Illinois programs comprising Sample #1 averaged 3.35 on the four Staff Qualifications items. The national sample comprising Sample #2 averaged 2.79 on these four items.

Many of the programs participating in Sample #1 and Sample #2 did not receive a copy of the instrument prior to the administration of the scale by a trained assessor. It is anticipated that as the PAS is used broadly, the percentage of programs being rated at a level 1 on items will decrease as administrators will be better prepared with the necessary documentation for each indicator.

When looking at the national norms for Sample #2 detailed in Table 3, it should also be noted that the percentage of NAEYC-accredited programs in this sample was 31%, considerably higher than the overall national percentage of accredited programs, which is only 7%. The Total PAS Score and individual item mean scores no doubt reflect this concentration of higher quality programs.

Internal consistency. The degree of coherence of items included on the *Program Administration Scale*, its internal consistency, was determined through computation of Cronbach's Alpha coefficient. Coefficient alpha for the total scale for Sample #1 was .85 and for Sample #2 it was .86, indicating that the PAS has acceptable internal consistency among items.

Distinctiveness of the subscales. The 10 subscales were correlated to determine the extent to which they measured distinct, though somewhat related, aspects of early childhood administration.

Subscale intercorrelations for Sample #1 ranged from .09 to .63, with a median value of .33. Subscale intercorrelations for Sample #2 ranged from .04 to .72, with a median value of .33. The data analyses confirm that the subscales, for the most part, measure distinct characteristics of organizational administration. Table 4 reports the results of the Pearson's *r* correlational analysis for Sample #2.

Table 4. Subscale Intercorrelations – Sample #2

Subscale	2	3	4	5	6	7	8	9	10
1. Human Resources Development	.40	.44	.40	.16	.24	.37	.42	.18	.04
2. Personnel Cost and Allocation		.39	.72	.60	.71	.44	.42	.26	.18
3. Center Operations			.32	.19	.27	.45	.52	.20	.16
4. Child Assessment				.15	.28	.31	.33	.17	.10
5. Fiscal Management					.33	.39	.35	.49	.13
6. Program Planning and Evaluation						.38	.34	.16	.19
7. Family Partnerships							.50	.11	.17
8. Marketing and Public Relations								.16	.17
9. Technology									.17
10. Staff Qualifications									--

Item intercorrelations were also calculated using Pearson's *r*. These coefficients ranged from .02 to .78 for Sample #1 and .01 to .58 for Sample #2, confirming that the individual items on the PAS measure somewhat distinct but related characteristics of organizational administration.

Inter-rater reliability. Inter-rater reliability, the degree to which the assessor's item scores match the PAS anchors' scores, was determined during a four-day training on the use of the instrument. Using a videotape of the entire interview protocol, assessors were rated on how often they matched the PAS anchor's scores within 1 point for each item. For Sample #1 individual assessor's inter-rater reliability scores ranged from 81% to 95% agreement. Overall inter-rater reliability was 90% for the eight assessors used in Sample #1. Inter-rater reliability for all certified PAS assessors gathering data for Sample #2 ranged from 86% to 100% agreement with an overall average of 94%.

Differentiating programs. In order to determine if the *Program Administration Scale* adequately differentiates programs of varying quality, analysis of variance procedures were employed. NAEYC accreditation status was used as a measure of program quality. Those programs that were currently accredited by NAEYC were presumed to be of higher quality than those that were not accredited. Analysis of variance offers an empirical test of whether the PAS can differentiate programs based on their accreditation status.

Table 5 provides a summary of the ANOVA for Sample #2. The results provide confirmatory evidence that the PAS can adequately differentiate programs based on level of quality. Those programs that were accredited had significantly higher Total PAS Scores ($M = 85.68$, $SD = 21.97$) than those that were not accredited ($M = 73.18$, $SD = 24.10$). The Total PAS Scores for this analysis were based on 23 items (possible range 23–161), since all centers did not include the positions of Teacher and Assistant Teacher/Aide as part of the teaching staff. Similar results were found in the analysis of Sample #1 data ($M = 92.12$ versus $M = 72.06$).

Table 5. Analysis of Variance by NAEYC Accreditation Status – Sample #2

	Sum of Squares	df	Mean Square	F	p<
Between groups	1467.28	1	1467.28	27.03	.0001
Within groups	213922.70	394	542.96		
Total	**2638331.00**	**396**			

Table 6 reports the six items for Sample #2 that were found to be most strongly associated with accreditation status.

Table 6. Rank Ordering of Items Associated with NAEYC Accreditation Status – Sample #2

Item	Not accredited	Accredited	
	M	*M*	*p <*
Assessment in Support of Learning	4.12	5.59	.001
Teacher Qualifications	2.24	3.58	.001
Assistant Teacher/Aide Qualifications	3.14	4.07	.001
Benefits	1.70	2.61	.001
Technological Resources	3.44	4.31	.001
Lead Teacher Qualifications	2.35	3.12	.001

Analysis of variance procedures were also used to determine whether programs of varying sizes scored differently on the *Program Administration Scale*. An analysis of the Sample #1 data found that for 23 of the 25 items, there were no statistically significant differences based on program size (small, medium, large). For the 67 programs included in that sample, the item Staffing Patterns and Scheduling had higher scores in smaller programs and the item Accounting Practices had higher scores in larger programs ($p < .05$).

The results for Sample #2 were somewhat different. Results of an ANOVA and post hoc tests indicate that there were significant differences in Total PAS Scores based on program size with large programs ($M = 83.57$) and medium-size programs ($M = 77.06$), scoring significantly higher on the overall PAS than small programs ($M = 74.03$, $F = 5.77$, $p < .01$). The specific items differentiating programs by size relate, for the most part, to infrastructure capacity. Larger programs are more likely to have formal systems in place for budget planning, facilities management, accounting practices, strategic planning, and program evaluation.

Analysis of variance procedures were also conducted to understand whether programs that received Head Start funding scored differently on the PAS than programs that did not receive Head Start funding. Results of an ANOVA indicate that Total PAS Scores did not significantly differ between programs receiving Head Start funding ($M = 80.37$) and those that did not receive Head Start funding ($M = 76.81$, $F = 2.08$, $p = .15$).

Analysis of variance procedures were again undertaken to understand whether programs that received state prekindergarten funding scored differently on the PAS than programs that did not receive this funding. Results of an ANOVA indicate that Total PAS Scores did significantly differ, with state-funded prekindergarten programs scoring, on average, 83.67 and programs not receiving this funding scoring 76.63 ($F = 7.11$, $p < .01$). In general, programs receiving state prekindergarten funding tended to have higher staff qualifications, better benefits, and better systems for screening and identification of special needs.

Additional analysis was undertaken to determine whether PAS scores differed by program type (legal auspice). Results of an ANOVA revealed that nonprofit programs had significantly higher Total PAS Scores ($M = 81.83$) than for-profit programs ($M = 65.98$, $F = 33.95$, $p < .001$).

Concurrent validity. Concurrent validity for the PAS was determined by a correlational analysis with two other instruments that measure early childhood organizational effectiveness: the Professional Growth subscale of the *Early Childhood Work Environment Survey* (ECWES) and the Parents and Staff subscale of the *Early Childhood Environment Rating Scale–Revised*. As Table 7 shows, the moderate correlations with both the ECERS–R Parents and Staff subscale and ECWES Professional Growth subscale indicate that the PAS measures related but not redundant characteristics of organizational quality.

Table 7. Correlation of PAS Subscales with the ECERS–R Parents and Staff Subscale and the ECWES Professional Growth Subscale – Sample #1 ($N = 67$)

PAS Subscale	ECERS-R	ECWES
Human resources development	.33	.42
Personnel cost and allocation	.45	.42
Center operations	.33	.32
Child assessment	.29	.05
Fiscal management	.47	.40
Program planning and evaluation	.36	.24
Family partnerships	.34	.43
Marketing and public relations	.10	.05
Technology	.32	.38
Staff qualifications	.26	.35
PAS Total	**.53**	**.52**

The results of the reliability and validity study support the conclusion that the *Program Administration Scale* has achieved all seven psychometric criteria: it measures somewhat distinct but related administrative practices of early childhood programs; can differentiate between low- and high-quality programs as measured by NAEYC accreditation status; is applicable for use in different types of programs; can be used by programs of varying sizes; demonstrates good internal consistency; has good inter-rater reliability; and is easy to score and use as a tool to support program improvement efforts.

Related Research

The *Program Administration Scale* has been used in several studies evaluating the quality of center-based leadership and management practices, statewide quality rating and improvement systems, and state professional development and director credentialing systems. The following are selected studies that provide evidence of the predictive validity of the PAS and confirm the utility of the instrument for measuring quality, monitoring improvements, and benchmarking change in organizational practices.

Study #1. Lower and Cassidy (2007) conducted a study of 30 centers in North Carolina to assess the relationship between program administration practices, staff's perceptions of organizational climate, and classroom quality. The PAS was used to assess the quality of administrative practices; the ECWES was used to measure organizational climate; and observations of two classrooms at each center using the ECERS–R were conducted to assess the quality of the classroom learning environment.

Internal consistency for the PAS was .88. Mean item scores ranged from 2.87 to 5.19. Internal consistency of the ECERS–R was .83; scores ranged from 3.90 to 6.00. The results of the data analysis found a dynamic relationship among program leadership and management practices, teachers' perceptions of their work environment reflected in its organizational climate, and how those variables relate to the classroom practices experience by children.

Program administration, as measured by the PAS, was significantly related to classroom global quality. The Pearson's r correlation revealed a statistically significant moderate correlation between PAS scores and ECERS–R scores ($r = .29, p < .05$). The researchers also found that directors with a four-year degree scored significantly higher on the PAS ($M = 3.24$) than directors without a four-year degree ($M = 2.49$). The study suggests that program administration practices and organizational climate are important variables related to the quality of classroom learning environments.

Study #2. The McCormick Center for Early Childhood Leadership at National Louis University, in collaboration with the Chicago Department of Family and Support Services, conducted a study to examine how administrative practices in Head Start programs are related to classroom quality (MCECL, 2010c). The research also looked at director qualifications in Head Start programs to understand how specific dimensions of director qualifications are related to the quality of Head Start administrative practices and the quality of the classroom learning environment. The PAS was used as a measure of the quality of administrative practices and the ECERS–R was used as a measure of classroom quality. Data were collected in 2006 in 452 Head Start classrooms in 138 centers in Chicago.

Multiple regression analyses, controlling for length of day, number of teachers, annual turnover rate, lead teacher qualifications, and child enrollment were conducted to understand whether higher PAS scores predicted higher ECERS–R scores. Mean PAS scores for this sample were calculated at 3.42 with scores ranging from 1.58 to 5.88 while mean ECERS–R scores were calculated at 4.20 with scores ranging from 2.41 to 6.12. The results of the data analysis revealed that administrative quality accounted for 26% of the variance in Head Start classroom quality ($t = 3.62, p = .0001$), demonstrating that administrative practices, as measured by the PAS, strongly influenced the quality of care that children receive in their classrooms.

To address the second research question regarding director qualifications, an overall PAS score was calculated using all PAS items except staff qualifications. Correlations were then conducted between the different dimensions of director qualifications and PAS scores. Correlations revealed that higher quality administrative practices were associated with directors who had a master's degree ($r = .22, p < .01$), had completed more management coursework ($r = .20, p < .01$), and had made more professional contributions during the past three years ($r = .25, p < .01$).

Finally, the researchers looked specifically at the relationship between directors' qualifications, as measured by the PAS, and classroom quality, as measured by the ECERS–R. The results of the data analysis found that higher classroom quality was associated with directors who had a bachelor's degree or higher ($r = .22$, $p < .01$), had completed 24 or more semester hours of early childhood coursework ($r = .19$, $p = .02$), and had made at least four professional contributions during the past three years ($r = .20$, $p = .01$).

Study #3. In 2006, researchers at the National Center for Children and Families at Teachers College, Columbia University were commissioned to propose a uniform and comprehensive performance measurement system for all publicly funded early childhood programs in New York City (Kagan et al., 2008). Two of the measures used in the citywide pilot were the PAS and the ECERS–R. The total sample included 130 classrooms from 37 Head Start, community-based child care, and universal prekindergarten programs.

The Average PAS Item Scores for the 35 sites that completed a PAS assessment was 3.87. Scores ranged from 2.28 to 5.28. Head Start programs in the sample scored highest with an Average PAS Item Score of 4.59. Community-based child care programs scored lowest with an Average PAS Item Score of 3.34. Results of the data analysis showed a correlation between the PAS and the ECERS–R scores ($r = .52$, $p < .01$).

To confirm that the two measures capture distinct dimensions of quality, factor analysis was employed. Two major factors emerged from the analysis. The first factor exclusively included items from the ECERS–R, while the second only included items from the PAS, indicating that these two instruments capture distinct elements of program quality. The researchers' recommendation was that New York City's unified performance measurement system should use both measures; program administration and classroom quality are both important elements of a well-functioning program.

Study #4. An evaluation of Arkansas' professional development support system was conducted by KeyStone Research Corporation using the PAS as one of the tools to measure the quality of centers that had received professional development support through the Arkansas State University Childhood Services (Miller & Bogatova, 2007). Trained PAS assessors gathered data from 169 early care and education programs.

The results of the evaluation showed that the PAS differentiated the quality of administrative practices between programs classified as meeting minimal licensing requirements, those that met the state accreditation standards classified as Arkansas Quality Approval (QA) programs, and those that met state prekindergarten standards classified as Arkansas Better Chance (ABC) programs. In 24 of the 25 PAS items, QA and ABC programs out-performed programs classified as meeting minimum licensing standards. The Average PAS Item Score for the QA and/or ABC programs was 4.47, compared to 3.12 for those programs classified as meeting minimum licensing requirements ($p < .001$). The study also found statistically significant differences in PAS item scores between nonprofit and for-profit programs ($p < .001$).

Study #5. The McCormick Center for Early Childhood Leadership conducted a study to examine the early childhood program characteristics associated with utilization of the Illinois Great START (Strategies to Attract and Retain Teachers) wage supplement initiative (MCECL, 2007). Forty Illinois Department of Human Services site-contracted early care and education centers were included in the sample; 20 that had a high utilization of Great START funds and 20 that did not use or had a low utilization of these funds. The ECERS–R was used to measure the quality of 70 preschool classrooms in the sample; the PAS was used to measure the quality of leadership and management practices of the 40 programs included in the study.

The results of the data analysis revealed that in preschool classrooms, notable differences in the level of program quality were found as measured by the ECERS–R. Those centers classified as high utilization of Great START funds consistently demonstrated higher quality teaching practices ($p < .05$). In 22 of the 25 PAS items, the Total PAS Score, and the Average PAS Item Score, there were notable differences in the quality of administrative practices between those centers classified as high versus low utilization of Great START funds. Those classified as high utilization consistently demonstrated higher leadership and management practices. Statistically significant differences ($p < .05$) were found between the two groups in five items: Compensation, Screening and Identification of Special Needs, Strategic Planning, Lead Teacher Qualifications, and Assistant Teacher/Aide Qualifications.

Study #6. Researchers at the Human Development Institute at the University of Kentucky conducted a study to assess the impact of the Kentucky Professional Development Framework on classroom quality and child outcomes (Rous et al., 2008). The PAS was one of several different instruments used to collect data and inform the researchers and state policymakers about the effectiveness of the professional development system and the organizational factors that support or impede quality practices. The sample included 227 programs including Head Start, child care, and public prekindergarten.

In looking at the specific factors that impact early childhood professionals' ability to participate in professional development activities, the researchers found that administrators who worked with teachers who utilized Professional Development Plans as part of the state's Professional Development Framework scored significantly higher on the PAS item Staff Development ($t = 2.67$, $p < .01$). Teachers felt more supported by their administrators when they used Professional Development Plans. The researchers conclude that a supportive administrator combined with teacher experience and education, the use of Professional Development Plans by teachers, and the number of self-selected trainings attended by teachers had the highest impact on classroom quality scores as measured by the ECERS–R and the Early Language and Literacy Classroom Observation (ELLCO).

The results of the data analysis also surfaced statistically significant relationships between the PAS item Staff Development and the ELLCO Literacy Environment Checklist ($r = .28$, $p < .01$) and the average ECERS–R score ($r = .20$, $p < .05$). A similar significant relationship surfaced between the PAS item Supervision and Performance Appraisal and the ELLCO Literacy Environment Checklist ($r = .20$, $p < .05$) and the average ECERS–R score ($r = .20$, $p < .05$).

Study #7. Launched in 2008, the Tennessee Early Childhood Program Administrator Credential (TECPAC) is the recognition awarded to center directors who have demonstrated specific competencies for effective leadership and management through formal academics, experience, and portfolio assessment. Each year the Tennessee State University's Center of Excellence for Learning Sciences conducts an evaluation of the credential. The PAS is used as a pre- and post-assessment to measure changes in program quality for the administrators who are awarded the credential. (The Staff Qualifications subscale is not included in the evaluation data as that information is gathered elsewhere.)

The results of the 2009–10 evaluation show that 93% of the credential completers and 100% of the credential specialists felt the PAS was a beneficial tool for supporting program growth. Changes in mean item scores ranged from .02 (Benefits) to 3.00 points (Staff

Orientation), with a mean item improvement of 1.81 points. The most significant changes were related to the topics included in the credential training (Mietlicki, 2010).

Study #8. Researchers at the University of Arkansas' Partners for Inclusive Communities conducted an assessment of the state's Better Beginnings Quality Rating and Improvement System (QRIS) (McKelvey et al., 2010). The PAS is one of the required assessments used in Better Beginnings to achieve a quality rating. The four PAS items that comprise the Staff Qualifications subscale are not included in the Better Beginnings QRIS. Also Item 5 (Benefits) and Item 6 (Staffing Patterns and Scheduling) are assessed but not counted in a program's overall score.

Using data collected as part of the Evaluation of the Arkansas Early Childhood Professional Development System, the evaluation team compared the original scoring with the Better Beginnings scoring of the PAS. They found the correlations between the Better Beginnings PAS, the Environment Rating Scales, and the Arnett Caregiver Interaction Scales were weaker than with the original scoring of the PAS. The original PAS scoring was significantly related to teacher behaviors that support children's cognitive development and school readiness ($p < .01$). The Better Beginnings PAS scoring was not. These behaviors include engaging the children with open-ended questions and encouraging children in the use of symbolic/literacy materials, numbers and spatial concepts, and problem solving. The researchers state that the omitted PAS items may impact the measures' usefulness for Better Beginnings and recommend re-introducing the items that have been excluded from Better Beginnings.

Using the Better Beginnings scoring of the PAS, the evaluation team sought to determine whether cut scores for the system were meaningful. Better Beginnings' Levels 1 and 2 do not require PAS assessments while Level 3 requires a minimum score of 4.00. The researchers found that programs scoring lower than 4.00 on the scale have teachers who are less sensitive, more detached, and less supportive of socio-emotional development, and have classrooms with lower overall global environmental quality ratings.

Study #9. Arend (2010) investigated the human resource management practices of early childhood directors and the relationship between directors' level of management training and the quality of human resource management practices. The study used nine items from the PAS related to human resource issues—Staff Orientation, Staff Development, Supervision and Performance Appraisal, Compensation, Benefits, Staffing Patterns and Scheduling, Internal Communications, Program Evaluation, and Strategic Planning. The sample comprised 119 directors from five states. Data were collected electronically via a self-report questionnaire.

The results of the data analysis revealed the strongest management practices in the area of Supervision and Performance Appraisal and the weakest in the areas of Strategic Planning and Benefits. The majority of scores fell in the minimal to good range with none of the median scale scores greater than good.

Significant differences were also found among directors with varying levels of management coursework in six of the nine areas examined. In all of the post-hoc comparisons, directors with more management coursework scored higher than those with fewer management credits. In six of these areas, the differences reached statistical significance ($p < .01$).

Study #10. A study was conducted to discern differences in the quality of classroom learning environments, teacher-child interactions, organizational climate, leadership and management practices, staff turnover, and accreditation status as the result of a comprehensive professional development and quality enhancement initiative. Nine child care centers associated with well-established social service agencies in Chicago participated in the study, which spanned four years. The PAS was used to assess changes in the quality of leadership and management practices.

The intervention, conducted by the Center for Urban Research and Learning at Loyola University, included on-site technical assistance as well as a variety of professional development supports for teaching and administrative staff at the centers. The results of the data analysis show that there were notable improvements in program quality in the early childhood centers that participated in this project. The centers consistently demonstrated higher quality teaching practices (as measured by the Environment Rating Scales), a more positive work climate (as measured by the ECWES), and improved leadership and management practices (as measured by the PAS) in 2006 compared to 2002. The centers also experienced a significant decrease in the rate of annual turnover among teaching staff (Bloom & Talan, 2006).

With respect to the PAS, the results of a paired t-test statistical analysis revealed that in five of the ten subscales, the pre-post differences were statistically significant ($p < .05$). In 20 of the 25 PAS items, there were improvements in the quality of administrative practices as measured by the PAS between 2002 and 2006. In 12 of the items, these changes were statistically significant ($p < .05$). The Average PAS Item Score increased from 3.63 in 2002 to 4.72 in 2006 ($p < .05$).

This positive finding, however, masks significant differences in the magnitude of the changes in leadership and management practices at the nine centers. While the Average PAS Item Score increased between 2002 and 2006 at each of the centers assessed, at four of the centers the Average PAS Item Score increased by 33% or more. At one center, the Average PAS Item Score improved by 67%.

Study #11. Quality New York, a NAEYC accreditation facilitation project, is a comprehensive program improvement model that includes two types of support for participating program—group support activities and individualized on-site support. In an effort to better understand the impact of support on the quality of early childhood classroom and administrative practices, the Center for Assessment and Policy Development collected data from 11 early care and education programs that had participated in the Quality New York project for at least 18 months and had been identified as having substantial weaknesses (Stephens, 2009). The evaluation included repeated assessments using the ECERS–R and the PAS. Baseline Average PAS Item Scores ranged from 2.14 to 5.59. On average, programs had more than seven items scoring 2.00 or less.

The results of the study found that both individualized support through on-site consultation and group support through workshops and network meetings contributed to quality improvements, but in different ways. Individualized consultation contributed to greater improvements in the program's classroom learning environments, as measured by the ECERS–R. Group support was strongly associated with improvement in program administration and operations, as measured by the PAS. When examined together in a multiple regression analysis, both types of support were associated with decreased variability in the quality of the classrooms.

On average, programs improved their PAS scores by 2 or more points on just over six items. The researchers state that just as important as the improvements in specific areas of administration were changes in directors' understanding of their own leadership role. They became better organized and more focused, recognizing areas of administrative practice they needed to work on.

Multiple regressions that controlled for the initial PAS score and included the hours per month that the staff participated in professional development workshops and director meetings were statistically significant in predicting change in PAS scores and in the number of PAS items scored as high, explaining 60% and 58% respectively of the variance in these measures of program improvement. Additionally, the teaching staff's participation in professional development was strongly associated with improvements in their center's PAS scores. The study concludes that as directors gain greater understanding of their leadership and managerial roles in supervision and quality improvement, they take advantage of more professional development opportunities for their staff.

In Sum

The results of the eleven studies briefly described in the preceding section provide compelling evidence that the PAS is a reliable, valid instrument that approaches early childhood program quality from a different perspective than assessments focusing exclusively on the classroom learning environment or teacher-child interactions. The consensus appears to be that multiple measures generate a more comprehensive and refined picture of overall program quality. The *Program Administration Scale* is particularly useful in highlighting organizational strengths, pinpointing areas in need of improvement, and guiding administrators to make incremental changes that benefit staff, parents, and children.

References and Resources

Arend, L. (2010, October). *Filling the void: A call for educational administration preparation specific to early childhood leaders.* Paper presented at the annual conference of the University Council for Educational Administration, New Orleans.

Arnett, J. (1989). Caregivers in day care centers: Does training matter? *Journal of Applied Developmental Psychology, 10*(4), 541–552.

Barnett, W. S. (2003, March). *Better teachers, better preschools: Student achievement linked to teacher qualifications* (Issue 2). New Brunswick, NJ: National Institute for Early Education Research.

Bella, J. (2008, July/August). Improving leadership and management practices: One step at a time. *Exchange,* 6–10.

Bella, J., & Bloom, P. J. (2003). *Zoom: The impact of early childhood leadership training on role perceptions, job performance, and career decisions.* Wheeling, IL: McCormick Center for Early Childhood Leadership, National Louis University.

Bertachi, J. (1996, October/November). Relationship-based organizations. *Zero to Three Bulletin, 17*(2), 2–7.

Bloom, P. J. (2010). *Measuring work attitudes in the early childhood setting: Technical manual for the Early Childhood Job Satisfaction Survey and the Early Childhood Work Environment Survey.* Wheeling, IL: McCormick Center for Early Childhood Leadership, National Louis University.

Bloom, P. J. (2004). Leadership as a way of thinking. *Zero to Three, 25*(2), 21–26.

Bloom, P. J. (2000). *Circle of influence: Implementing shared decision making and participative management.* Lake Forest, IL: New Horizons.

Bloom, P. J. (1996). The quality of work life in NAEYC accredited and non-accredited early childhood programs. *Early Education and Development, 7*(4), 301–317.

Bloom, P. J., Hentschel, A., & Bella, J. (2010). *A great place to work: Creating a healthy organizational climate.* Lake Forest, IL: New Horizons.

Bloom, P. J., & Sheerer, M. (1992). The effect of leadership training on child care program quality. *Early Childhood Research Quarterly, 7*(4), 579–594.

Bloom, P. J., & Talan, T. N. (2006, October). *Changes in program quality associated with participation in a professional development initiative.* Wheeling, IL: McCormick Center for Early Childhood Leadership, National Louis University.

Burchinal, M., Cryer, D., Clifford, R., & Howes, C. (2002). Caregiver training and classroom quality in child care centers. *Applied Developmental Science, 6*(1), 2–11.

Center for the Child Care Workforce. (1998). *Creating better child care jobs: Model work standards.* Washington, DC: Author.

Cleveland, G. H., & Hyatt, D. (2002). Child care workers' wages: New evidence on returns to education, experience, job tenure, and auspice. *Journal of Population Economics, 15*(3), 575–597.

Cochran, M. (2007). Caregiver and teacher compensation. *Zero to Three, 28*(1), 42–47.

Cornille, T., Mullis, R., Mullis, A., & Shriner, M. (2006). An examination of child care teachers in for-profit and nonprofit child care centers. *Early Child Development and Care, 176*(6), 631–641.

Cost, Quality, and Child Outcomes Study Team. (1995). *Cost, quality, and child outcomes in child care centers.* Denver: Department of Economics, University of Colorado at Denver.

Culkin, M. L. (2000). *Managing quality in young children's programs: The leader's role.* New York: Teachers College Press.

Early Childhood Community Development Center. (2010, June). *Mentoring pairs for child care (MPCC) data brief.* St. Catherines, ON, Canada: Author.

Fowler, S., Bloom, P. J., Talan, T. N., Beneke, S., & Kelton, R. (2008). *Who's caring for the kids? The status of the early childhood workforce in Illinois.* Wheeling, IL: McCormick Center for Early Childhood Leadership, National Louis University.

Gratz,R., & Claffey, A. (1996). Adult health in child care: Health status, behaviors, and concerns of teachers, directors, and family child care providers. *Early Childhood Research Quarterly, 11*, 243–267.

Halle, T., Vick Whittaker, J. E., & Anderson, R. (2010). *Quality in early childhood care and education settings: A compendium of measures* (2nd ed.). Washington, DC: Child Trends.

Harms, T., Clifford, R., & Cryer, D. (2005). *Early Childhood Environment Rating Scale–Revised.* New York: Teachers College Press.

Hemmeter, M., Joseph, G., Smith, B., & Sandall, S. (Eds.). (2001). *DEC recommended practices program assessment: Improving practices for young children with special needs and their families.* Longmont, CO: Sopris West.

Herzenberg, S., Price, M., & Bradley, D. (2005). *Losing ground in early childhood education: Declining workforce qualifications in an expanding industry, 1979–2004.* Harrisburg, PA: Keystone Research Center.

Hyun, E. (1998). *Making sense of Developmentally and Culturally Appropriate Practice (DCAP) in early childhood education.* New York: Peter Lang.

Kagan, S. L., & Bowman, B. (Eds.). (1997). *Leadership in early care and education.* Washington, DC: National Association for the Education of Young Children.

Kagan, S. L., Brooks-Gunn, J., Westheimer, M., Tarrant, K., Cortazar, A., Johnson, A., Philipsen, N., & Pressman, A. (2008). *New York City early care and education unified performance measurement system: A pilot study.* New York: National Center for Children and Families.

Kagan, S. L., Kauerz, K., & Tarrant, K. (2008). *The early care and education teaching workforce at the fulcrum: An agenda for reform.* New York: Teachers College Press.

Lower, J. K., & Cassidy, D. J. (2007, Winter). Child care work environments: The relationship with learning environments. *Journal of Research in Childhood Education, 22*(2), 189–204.

McCormick Center for Early Childhood Leadership. (2010a, Summer). Connecting the dots: Director qualifications, instructional leadership practices, and learning environments in early childhood programs. *Research Notes.* Wheeling, IL: National Louis University.

McCormick Center for Early Childhood Leadership. (2010b, Spring). A window on early childhood administrative practices. *Research Notes*. Wheeling, IL: National Louis University.

McCormick Center for Early Childhood Leadership. (2010c, Winter). Head Start administrative practices, director qualifications, and links to classroom quality. *Research Notes*. Wheeling, IL: National Louis University.

McCormick Center for Early Childhood Leadership. (2008, Summer). Professional development: The landscape of opportunity in early care and education. *Research Notes*. Wheeling, IL: National Louis University.

McCormick Center for Early Childhood Leadership. (2007, Spring). Program characteristics associated with utilization of early childhood professional development funding. *Research Notes*. Wheeling, IL: National Louis University.

McKelvey, L., Chapin-Critz, M., Johnson, B., Bokony, P., Conners-Burrow, N., & Whiteside-Mansell, L. (2010). *Better Beginnings: Evaluating Arkansas' path to better child outcomes*. Little Rock, AR: Partners for Inclusive Communities.

Means, K. M., & Pepper, A. (2010). *Best practices of accreditation facilitation projects: A framework for program improvement using NAEYC early childhood program standards and accreditation criteria*. Washington, DC: National Association for the Education of Young Children.

Mietlicki, C. (2010, October). *Tennessee Early Childhood Program Administrator Credential: Year two evaluation report*. Nashville: Tennessee Early Childhood Training Alliance, Tennessee State University.

Miller, J. A., & Bogatova, T. (2007). *Early care and education workforce development initiatives: Program design, implementation, and outcomes*. Erie, PA: KeyStone Research Corporation.

National Association for the Education of Young Children. (2010). *A conceptual framework for early childhood professional development: A position statement* (Rev. ed.). Washington, DC: Author.

National Association for the Education of Young Children. (2007). *NAEYC early childhood program standards and accreditation criteria: The mark of quality in early childhood education* (Rev. ed.). Washington, DC: Author.

National Professional Development Center on Inclusion. (2008). *Professional development 1-2-3 planning guide*. Chapel Hill: FPG Child Development Center, University of North Carolina.

National School-Age Care Alliance. (1998). *NSACA standards for quality school-age care*. Boston: Author.

Phillips, D., Mekos, D., Scarr, S., McCartney, K., & Abbott-Shim, M. (2000). Within and beyond the classroom door: Assessing quality in child care centers. *Early Childhood Research Quarterly, 15*(4), 475–496.

Rohacek, M., Adams, G., & Kisker, E. (2010). *Understanding quality in context: Child care centers, communities, markets, and public policy*. Washington, DC: Urban Institute.

Rous, B., Grove, J., Cox, M., Townley, K., & Crumpton, G. (2008). *The impact of the Kentucky Professional Development Framework on child care, Head Start, and preschool classroom quality and child outcomes*. Lexington: Human Development Institute, University of Kentucky.

Smith, M., Dickinson, D., Sangeorge, A., & Anastasopoulos, L. (2002). *Early language and literacy classroom observation.* Newton, MA: Paul Brooks.

Stephens, S. A. (2009, August). *Quality New York: Assessment of its contributions to program improvement in early care and education programs in New York City.* New York: Center for Assessment and Policy Development. Available at www.capd.org/pubfiles/pub-2009-08-01.pdf

Talan, T. N. (2010, May/June). Distributive leadership: Something new or something borrowed? *Exchange,* 8–12.

Talan, T. N. (2007). *Roots and wings: Portrait of an early childhood learning organization* (doctoral dissertation). National Louis University, Wheeling, Illinois.

Torquati, J. C., Raikes, H., & Huddleston-Casas, C. A. (2007). Teacher education, motivation, compensation, workplace support, and links to quality of center-based child care and teachers' intention to stay in the early childhood profession. *Early Childhood Research Quarterly, 22*(2), 261–275.

Vu, J., Jeon, H., & Howes, C. (2008). Formal education, credential, or both: Early childhood program classroom practices. *Early Education and Development, 19*(3), 479–504.

Whitebook, M., Gomby, D., Bellm, D., Sakai, L., & Kipnis, F. (2009). *Preparing teachers of young children: The current state of knowledge, and a blueprint for the future.* Berkeley, CA: Center for the Study of Child Care Employment, Institute for Research on Labor and Employment, University of California at Berkeley.

Whitebook, M., Howes, C., & Phillips, D. (1990). *Who cares? Child care teachers and the quality of care in America: Final report of the National Child Care Staffing Study.* Oakland, CA: Child Care Employee Project.

Whitebook, M., Ryan, S., Kipnis, F., & Sakai, L. (2008, February). *Partnering for preschool: A study of center directors in New Jersey's mixed-delivery Abbott Program.* Berkeley: Center for the Study of Child Care Employment, Institute for Research on Labor and Employment, University of California at Berkeley.

About the Authors

Teri N. Talan, Ed.D., J.D.

Teri N. Talan is Director of Policy Initiatives for the McCormick Center for Early Childhood Leadership and Professor of Early Childhood Education at National Louis University in Wheeling, Illinois. She represents the McCormick Center in public policy forums and promotes action by state and national policymakers on early childhood education and program administration issues. She is also the editor of the Center's quarterly *Research Notes*. Previously, Dr. Talan was the Executive Director of a NAEYC-accredited early childhood program. She holds a law degree from Northwestern University as well as an Ed.D. in Adult and Continuing Education and an M.Ed. in Early Childhood Leadership and Advocacy from National Louis University. Dr. Talan's research interests are in the areas of early childhood leadership, workforce development, systems integration, and program quality evaluation. She is co-author of the *Business Administration Scale for Family Child Care* (BAS), *Escala de Evaluación de la Administración de Negocios* (Spanish BAS), and the report, *Who's Caring for the Kids? The Status of the Early Childhood Workforce in Illinois*.

Paula Jorde Bloom, Ph.D.

Paula Jorde Bloom is the Michael W. Louis Chair of the McCormick Center for Early Childhood Leadership and Professor of Early Childhood Education at National Louis University in Wheeling, Illinois. As one of the country's leading experts on early childhood leadership and program management issues, Dr. Bloom is a frequent keynote speaker at state, national, and international conferences and consultant to professional organizations and state agencies. She received her master's and doctoral degrees from Stanford University. She is the author of numerous journal articles and several widely read books including *Avoiding Burnout, Blueprint for Action, Circle of Influence, Making the Most of Meetings, Workshop Essentials, Measuring Work Attitudes, From the Inside Out, A Great Place to Work*, and *Leadership in Action*. Dr. Bloom's research interests are in the areas of organizational climate, occupational stress, job satisfaction, staff development, and other early childhood workforce issues. She is the author of the *Early Childhood Work Environment Survey* (ECWES) and the *Early Childhood Job Satisfaction Survey* (ECJSS).

Notes

Notes

Notes